ANUNNAKI GODS
THE SUMERIAN RELIGION
NEW STANDARD ZUIST EDITION

POCKET EDITION

Published from
Mardukite Borsippa HQ, San Luis Valley, Colorado
Founding Church of Mardukite Zuism,
Mardukite Academy & Systemology Society
for religious and educational purposes only.

ANUNNAKI GODS

THE SUMERIAN RELIGION

NEW STANDARD ZUIST EDITION

Developed by Joshua Free for the
Church of Mardukite Zuism

THE JOSHUA FREE IMPRINT
JFI PUBLICATIONS

© 2022, JOSHUA FREE

ISBN : 979-8-9864379-4-1

A special pocket version of
Sumerian Religion (Liber-50)
edited for founding the
Church of Mardukite Zuism

Pocket Paperback Edition — *July 2022*

Also available in hardcover as
"Sumerian Religion"

mardukite.com

The _Original_ Religion on Planet Earth

Long-lost secrets of ancient Mesopotamian
religion and Anunnaki mythology drawn from
cuneiform tablets are revealed to all in this
special pocket paperback edition of the
original Mardukite guide to the esoteric
archaeology of Sumer and Babylon.

Even if you think you already know all about the
Sumerian Anunnaki or StarGates of Babylon...

Here is a Master Key to the ancient mystic arts;
true knowledge concerning the powers and entities
that these arts are dedicated to; a working
relationship with these powers directly; and the
wisdom to co-exist "alongside" the gods, so as to
ever remain in the "favor" of Cosmic Law.

Unparalleled clarity of this revolutionary volume
make it worth 100-sars times its weight in lapis
lazuli and precious gold, offering Seekers what
may be the most critical and powerful religious,
spiritual or magical venture possible: a personal
relationship with the Anunnaki Gods — the
Divine Pantheon that launched a thousand
cultures and traditions throughout the world.

Here is the New Standard Zuist Edition of the
classic text by world renowned Joshua Free;
a special pocket paperback version of
"Sumerian Religion"
edited for the Church of Mardukite Zuism.

Other New Standard Zuist Editions:

Anunnaki Bible – The Cuneiform Scriptures

Anunnaki Rites – The Maqlu Ritual Book

TABLET OF CONTENTS

10TH ANNIVERSARY INTRODUCTION

by Joshua Free

The Mardukite Chamberlains (Mardukite Research Organization) completed its Year-1 cycle of work in early 2010—and those efforts culminated into an anthology first released as *"Necronomicon: The Anunnaki Bible"*—but which, for a recent solidification of our tradition as Mardukite Zuism, has also been published as *"The Complete Anunnaki Bible"*; and even a newly revised pocket-portable abridged format, *"Anunnaki Bible: The Cuneiform Scriptures (New Standard Zuist Edition),"* is available. That culmination of material has certainly earned its recognition as a critical staple and source book for a modern Mardukite spiritual revival, even now, over a decade later.

Although a necessary foundation to work from, completion of the Year-1 (2009) work proved to be only a beginning for the route that would carry and build a global underground spiritual movement, now, into the 2020's and beyond with a revitalized "religious brand" as *Mardukite Zuism* and its very effective *Systemology* of applied spiritual technology.

Much of this would not have been possible—or even coherently relevant—were it not for the pivotal Year-2 (2010) continuation of efforts made by "Chamberlains Alumni," those that dedicated another year of attention to the practical esoteric interpretation of the "*Anunnaki Bible*" and its background.

May 1 (Beltane) 2010, the "Council of Nabu-Tutu" (Alumni) oversaw publication of what would later become some of the widest circulating Mardukite materials on the planet: "*Liber-50*" (simultaneously released as "*Sumerian Religion*" and "*Gates of the Necronomicon*") and "*Liber-W*" ("*The Book of Marduk by Nabu*"). Combined with the "Tablet Catalogue" provided in the "*Anunnaki Bible*" source book, this arsenal of work proved to be essential for thousands of Seekers establishing a personal platform from the Mardukite paradigm on which to base an even higher reach on the Pathway...

ORIGINAL 2010 EDITION PREFACE

by Joshua Free

The quest of uncovering the true ancient and mystical arts carries a fundamental theme: establishment of true knowledge concerning the powers these arts are dedicated to and then a working relationship with these powers—or *entities*, as some are more likely to understand them. This is the true art of the "priest," "priestess," "mystic" and "wizard"—the one that pleases the "gods" in such a way so as to obtain "favor," but does not waste time in provoking malignant spirits at their Magic Circle—as does the "sorcerer"—and thus does not work a "magic" in fear for their lives at the mistaken utterance of an incantation.

On our journey to rediscover the most ancient writings, we are brought face to face with confronting traditions and spirito-mystical systems from the Ancient Near East, those born from the Sumerians—and then afterward extended to the developing cultures known as Akkadians, Chaldeo-Babylonians, Assyrians... and even the Egyptians are a part of this stream.

A continuing spread of the Anunnaki Tradition across Europe led to even more colorful and fanciful realizations of the primary "Olympian-archetype" for mythology all over the globe, but which was first realized and systematized in ancient

Mesopotamia—and especially in Babylon.

Ancient Sumerians referred to this race of *Sky Gods* as the *Anunnaki*. Their legacy and influence on planet Earth, and toward the cultivation of human civilization, is only recently reaching a threshold of "common knowledge." Of course, alongside this, an increased amount of "fluff" and "bullshit" has also appeared—and we have run into many individuals caught up in this, that either believe they *do* know something, or else are intentionally misguiding and contribute only to further misrepresentations of this lore now running rampant with many modern spiritual revivals, in New Age literature, on television and, of course, the web.

Given the restricted access to true "source material" for this research, the heavy expense of its acquisition, or obscure renderings and languages that it appears in, many of those in today's society are, themselves, simply uneducated enough to properly interpret and discern the data. Keep in mind, we are not dealing with a subject frequently treated in traditional school systems of the present era. This was, in fact, one of the reasons for establishing Mardukite Ministries (Mardukite Research Organization), far more than it was to extend a "mortal human devotion" to the specific deity in the Anunnaki pantheon named Marduk—but from which, we of course have drawn our name.

My current work and past years working with
Mardukite Chamberlains within this system has
been sufficient for me to know that these Anunnaki beings *are*, in fact, the "gods" appearing as
"divine representatives" throughout ancient cultures appearing on the planet. What's more, their
presence was later interpreted in the guise of "fairy
tales," a facet that seems to also carry remnants of
"folk magic" from ancient traditions into today.
Curiously, the "ceremonial magic" used by priests
and priestesses of long-lost eras, and even the self-
styled magicians of today, are really just working
with these same forces—but under some other
more recent guise, name or fragmentation. Should
all this be the case: the proper understanding and
establishment of our position with these beings—
this relationship—is perhaps one of the most paramount endeavors of this lifetime.

ORIGINAL 2010 EDITION FOREWORD

"Establishing a Relationship with Anunnaki Gods"
by Sarah Banas

Sleepless, yet not really quite awake. This world is a dream; we are players on a chessboard. The Matrix. A world within another world. We all know this; and still, we move aimlessly through life as if our actions have no consequences: that we are individuals, whose sole purpose is to live for ourselves. You have stayed awake many a night, staring at the ceiling and asking, "Why?" You felt it, you fought against it, this Machine—your material physical identity—that controls your movement; this Pendulum that never allows you a medium, always swinging you from one extreme to the next. And you allow it. How selfish has the race become that its' very existence has become a cancer to the planet? Do you even care anymore? Is only your material self—your temporary life—so important, that you must destroy everything in your path to prove your existence? A spoiled child who does not get what they want, so they throw a tantrum. Are you exhausted yet?

Humans are an empty shell of their former selves. Where once you walked with the gods—enjoyed a personal relationship with them—all you do now is pay lip service, demanding favors and requests; as if they cannot see your lies; as if they owe something to you. You fell in the same political and religious agendas as they did: the same paranoia; the lies; the fear; and the abuse. You have attacked each other, destroyed and brought each other to ruin. Your so-called prophets—"enlightened" —that you put on a pedestal to lead you, fail, because you have failed yourselves. Unlike the gods, you have refused to accept the consequences of your actions: you blame it on them—you have given up responsibility. Why? What happened to you?

Silently we wander. It never ceases to amaze me that humans want to be gods, and yet, when gods walk among you, you fail to see them. Unless, you do see them and purposely ignore them, because they are a threat to your own so-called divinity? And I am not talking of the hacks, the abusers who assimilate power and manipulate you—which, you so kindly allow—but the true gods: the silent ones. These are the writers, the artists, the musicians, who use the aesthetic arts to show you a world you know exists; and you feel it, but refuse to see it and acknowledge it.

You have gods on Earth today who are teachers, true religious leaders, students, store owners, who use leadership to teach you who to awaken your own divinity. You will never hear of them in the newspaper. You will rarely hear of their good deeds, their intentions, as they work behind the scenes, knowing the suffering and abuse they will sustain should they reveal themselves.

Just because the gods—the Anunnaki—do not show themselves in the way you want them to, does not mean they do not exist. It does not mean they do not hear your anger, or do not weep with you when you cry, or carry you when you no longer can walk. It does not mean that the gods do not share with you in your joy, or remind you of your gifts and talents when you yourself forget them, or inspire you when you have writer's block.

Politics. Even the divine Anunnaki did not escape such a disaster as politics. It is a game. The political debate between two or more opposing factions is not a bad endeavor. Wise judgment can always be exercised—such as with (the true story of) KA.IN and AB.EL. It is pride that eventually befalls all entities, the pride that sneaks in and corrupts the mind in all aspects (not just in politics), which becomes our destroyer.

The current state of the *Human Condition* faces such <u>politics</u>, even outside of the political system, that it uses to utterly implode on itself. There is just something about that word that can destroy the very core of anyone caught in it...

The gods feel as you do, they love, they cry, they are afraid: just like you.

They love being remembered once in a while, they love receiving gifts—and not as a *quid pro quo*, but as something you just wanted to do—and they love giving them, too. They tease, they poke fun, they laugh, and they enjoy. They have moments of weakness, and moments of strength. They can get spiteful when angry, they can get hurt when misunderstood or take the wrong way; they fear to lose you just as you fear to lose them... but on a much greater, deeper, and more loving level.

It must be a hard existence on the gods' part to be immortal, and have their very creation hate and spite their name, to be forgotten and abused... and still, carry on, take care of and try to help those same creations that hate them so dearly. They are our husbands and wives, our best friends, our lovers. They are our brothers and sisters, our children, our parents. They are us, they are with us, they are beside us. They love dearly, even if affection for each other was sometimes less than that. And even if we sometimes feel it's less, too.

No conventional theology will tell you that you can talk to a god or goddess as a friend, lover, mate, sibling or anything but a superior entity that you must prostrate yourself endlessly before them. I am telling you, in absolute Love, that you can. You can go with them to the movies, walk with them at the park, or pick flowers with them or feed them or they you. They have favorite colors, they cry during sad songs, they love to be held and they love to hold. I have told pagans that one god loves to play the harp, or that one enjoys paintings (or shiny things!); and they look at me with disbelief and—I daresay—annoyance for even suggesting that gods are anything but all powerful drones that do nothing but wait for prayers, demand absolute unquestionable devotion, and work all the time.

As with anything and anyone, treat them with love and respect, be honest with them, and they will do the exact same for you. Ask questions, walk with them, talk with them, just simply: Love them.

This planet, humanity, and everything intertwined is in need of healing. We can't do it alone, and it all starts with the Truth. Maybe it's time for us, "the gods who came down to earth" to lead, not only humanity, but to help the Gods who are beyond this realm to heal, too. The wars, the fighting, the distrust and anger between our groups has to end if they cannot set an example for us, we will set an example for them. *Won't you join us?*

To the followers of the three patriarchal religions: your god's name is the same as the one's we know… throw aside your pride and realize, you are not original. Your religion came from us. You worship Marduk, Enki and Enlil by a different name. So, why do you hate us? Are you not our brethren? And to the pagans: focus on the female, but never forget the male aspects of existence either. No true unity may exist with only half of a Twin. How can there be peace, if only half of the whole is respected?

Be an example for the rest: be the Gods of the Earth, be the Lucifer of life in Love once again, and show the world that the Gods never left. Show the world that the Gods are here, have been here, and will be here. We are Their representatives, so let's start acting like it. Isn't it time for the world to change? Isn't it time for Peace and Love to finally return?

—*In Nomine Enlil et Enki et Marduk Sancti.*

MARDUKITE

ZUISM

A BRIEF
INTRODUCTION

*According to the most ancient
historical records
written at the birth of our
modern civilization...**

432,000 YEARS AGO...*

a small population of advanced beings—called the <u>ANUNNAKI</u>—began developing the planet Earth for their purposes. These elite Self-Actualized spiritual beings resided on Earth in physical bodies, but found their forms inadequate for the physical labors required. Enter: the "Human Condition." Ancient "<u>cuneiform</u>" tablet writings from Sumerians and Babylonians of Mesopotamia are clear regarding the original creation and systematic programming of Humanity.

CUNEIFORM...

is the oldest known writing system used by scribes of ancient Babylon to record their wisdom and the history of humanity on <u>clay tablets</u>. "Cuneiform" is named for its style of wedge-shaped script formed by a <u>reed pen</u> called a "<u>stylus.</u>" Rather than an alphabet of letters, cuneiform is a system of "<u>signs</u>" representing "things" and "ideas." These may be combined to represent even more complex "signs."

---

* Version 1.1 – First published in 2019 as *Mardukite Zuism: A Brief Introduction* in booklet form.

Many concepts adopted for modern "Mardukite Zuism" are derived from cuneiform tablets. The ANUNNAKI introduced complex writing systems in order to program civilization and all parameters of Reality for the Human Condition. Legendary "Tablets of Destiny" (Divine Truth, supreme knowledge and cosmic power of the "gods") were first introduced to Humanity in the Babylonian narrative known best as the "Epic of Creation.

THE ARCANE TABLETS.

Ancient Babylonians used the Tablets of Destiny & Creation Epic to systematize all cosmic knowledge into a workable paradigm called "Mardukite Zuism"—a systemology received directly from the ANUNNAKI.

Paradigm : an all-encompassing standard or religion used to view the world and communicate reality.

Systemology : applied philosophies of Mardukite Zuism combined with personal spiritual techniques and technology ("Tech") that is effectively demonstrating systematic principles of a "paradigm."

THE EPIC OF CREATION.

Seven cuneiform tablets compose the ancient <u>Babylonian Epic of Creation</u>, named the <u>Enuma Eliš</u> by scholars after its opening lines. These seven tablets are the basis for what later traditions refer to as the "*Seven Days of Creation.*" The *Epic of Creation* tablets describe development of all existences with a Divine artistic perfection. The Enuma Eliš is the core example of religious literature from Babylon, which served as the basis for ancient "*Mardukite Zuism*"—the first true systematized religion in history.

THE SYSTEMOLOGY OF LIFE, UNIVERSES & EVERYTHING.

The *Arcane Tablets* describe the division of the ALL by the LAW, outside of which is but IN-FINITY. The *Epic of Creation* describes these activities as "mythology."

The Mardukite Systemology "Standard Model" uses the same information to demonstrates...

that <u>ALL</u> ("AN-KI") envelops both:
the <u>Spiritual Existences</u> ("AN")
and the <u>Physical Existences</u> ("KI")
divided by <u>Cosmic Law</u> and
connected by <u>Life-Awareness</u> ("ZU")
and beyond which is only the <u>Abyss</u>,
an <u>Infinity of Nothingness</u> ("ABZU").

ANCIENT SUMERIAN DEFINITIONS.

<u>ABZU</u> = "Abyss" ("Nothingness")
<u>ZU</u> = "Spiritual Life" ("Awareness")
<u>ANKI</u> = "All Existences" ("Existence")
<u>AN</u> = "Spiritual Universe" ("Heaven")
<u>KI</u> = "Physical Universe" ("Earth")

ALTERNATE MARDUKITE NEXGEN SYSTEMOLOGY DEFINITIONS.

<u>ABZU</u> = "Infinity of Nothingness"
<u>ZU</u> = "Awareness of Alpha Spirit"
<u>ANKI</u> = "The Standard Model"
<u>AN</u> = "Alpha Existence" ("Spiritual")
<u>KI</u> = "Beta Existence" ("Physical")

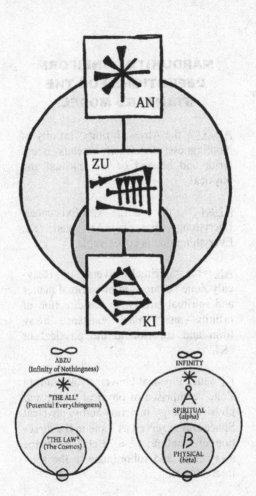

MARDUKITE CUNEIFORM DEFINITIONS FOR THE STANDARD MODEL.

<u>ABZU</u> = the Abyss; Infinity; Infinity of Nothingness; that which extends, is exterior and beyond of the spiritual and physical.

<u>ANKI</u> = the ALL; All Existences; Everything that is AN and KI; Everything that is conceivable.

<u>AN</u> = the "Spiritual Universe" or "Heavenly Zone" comprised of spiritual matter and spiritual energy, in the direction of Infinity—an "Alpha" existence away from and superior to the physical or "KI."

<u>KI</u> = the "Physical Universe" or "Earthly Zone" comprised of physical matter and physical energy in action across physical Space and observed as Time in the direction of Continuity—a "Beta" existence away from and subordinate to the spiritual or "AN."

ZU = "to know"; "knowingness";
"Awareness" or "consciousness"; spiritual energy and matter of AN that is
observed as "Lifeforce" in KI; "Spiritual
Life Energy"; the actual personal spiritual Identity or "Awareness" of Self as
Spirit which extends along a "line" from
the Spiritual Universe (AN) to the Physical Universe (KI).

THE TABLETS OF DESTINY &
BABYLONIAN CREATION EPIC.

The Absolute behind ALL Existence is referred
to on the *Tablets of Destiny* as the Infinity of
Nothingness. It is the only constant static of latent unmanifest potentiality of ALL and
Everythingness.

The LAW—Cosmic Law—is defined as the
Cosmic Dragon—TIAMAT—on "Epic of Creation" Tablets. She is the First Cause or
movement across a "Sea of Infinity." Later, the
LAW becomes a division between Spiritual Existence ("AN") and any Physical Universe
("KI"). The LAW—Tiamat—permeating ALL,
uses the *Tablets of Destiny* and then fixes the

systems of finite potential: The Systems of Manifestation—Substance, Motion and Awareness.

"Before heaven or earth are named," the formation and interaction of active existences —"substances" and "bodies" and "Life" and "gods"—creates turbulence and waves of action through space. The governing system of Cosmic Law—Tiamat—responds accordingly. She fixes the Tablets of Destiny to her "deputy"—a messenger wave action of the LAW named "Kingu" and sends him rippling out to "meet" the Anunnaki "gods."

The Anunnaki Assembly of "gods" prepare to battle The LAW. When none among them comes forth to engage, it is the Anunnaki "god" MARDUK that volunteers as hero to confront Kingu and Tiamat—but with a condition that the Anunnaki Assembly recognize him as "Chief of the Gods" upon his success.

When MARDUK approaches the LAW directly, he is flanked by Kingu and the "army of Ancient Ones." MARDUK is able to relinquish the Tablets of Destiny from Kingu. With the Tablets of Destiny, Marduk conquers a true understanding of Cosmic Law and thereby Tiamat.

THE TABLETS OF DESTINY
& SELF-HONESTY.

Marduk uses the Tablets of Destiny to discover "Self-Honesty" and Divine Knowledge governing "Cosmic Ordering"—systems dividing the "Spiritual Universe" (AN) from a "Physical Universe" (KI). The two universes are connected only by a stream of Spiritual Lifeforce Awareness that Sumerians called ZU. Wisdom from the Arcane Tablets is later passed down to and concealed by an ancient esoteric secret society in Babylon: the Scribes, High Priests and Priestesses of Mardukite Zuism.

Self-Honesty is a term describing an original "Alpha" state of clear knowingness and Self-directed beingness. "Self-Honesty" is the most basic and true expression of Self as "I-AM"— free of artificial attachments; reactive-response conditioning; and imposed or enforced programming as Reality for the Human Condition. Spiritual development in modern *Mardukite Zuism* is referred to as the "Pathway to Self-Honesty" and the "Gateway to Infinity." It is modeled directly from the Ancient Mystery Tradition observed at the Temples of Babylon.

THE KEY TO THE GATE.

"I will take my Blood—and with Bone—I will fashion a Race of Humans to keep Watch of the Gate. And from the Blood of Kingu I will create another Race of Humans to inhabit the Earth in service to the Gods—so shrines to the Anunnaki may be built and the temples filled. I will bind the Elder Gods to the Watchtowers; let them keep watch over the Gate of Abzu and the Gate of Tiamat and Gate of Kingu—and with a Key that shall be ever hidden, known to none, except only to my Mardukites." —MARDUK, *Enuma Elis, Creation Tablet VI*.

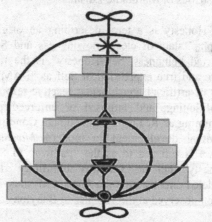

THE ANUNNAKI LADDER OF LIGHTS & BABYLONIAN GATEWAYS TO INFINITY.

ZIGGURAT TEMPLES in Babylonia—and throughout Mesopotamia—served to remind populations of the ZU connecting "Heaven" and "Earth."

Seven-stepped "levels" of the physical ZIG-GURAT TEMPLES of Babylonia—and seven corresponding Gates—represent spiritual levels of actualized Awareness; states of Self-purification (or "spiritual defragmentation") as they ascend in the direction of AN toward Infinity of Supreme Beingness—the Pathway of Self-Honesty—in imitation of the footsteps of the gods during their descent through the "spheres" or "Gates."

COSMOLOGY AND METAPHYSICS.

All Things in the Physical Universe are in motion—wave motions of "energy and matter in space measured as-and-across time." Continuity of the Physical Universe (KI) is divided by LAW and encompassed by the ALL (ANKI).

The direction of AN extends toward ABZU, an Infinity of Nothingness beyond effective existence.

The true <u>Alpha Self</u> is a source—the "spiritual cause" of "physical effects." It engages a <u>Self-determined WILL</u> from its "spiritual" <u>Alpha existence</u> to actualize Awareness for "physical" <u>Beta existence</u> experience as "Life."

USING ANCIENT WISDOM TO UNLOCK HUMAN POTENTIAL.

Communication of clear wisdom and true knowledge from Arcane Tablets is distorted as it passes through time and geography, diverse languages and authoritarian cultures using the "Power" to program the masses and fragment the Human Condition away from Self-Honesty.

Use of this ancient wisdom reveals the Keys to "<u>Cosmic Ordering</u>"—applying the highest Self-directed understanding of "cause-and-effect" sequences in the Physical Universe.

MARDUKITE ZUISM, SYSTEMOLOGY & SPIRITUALITY.

The Spiritual Universe (AN)—of metaphysical or spiritual energy and metaphysical or spiritual matter is not dependent on the Physical Universe (KI) to exist; the two are existentially independent of each other, maintaining a single channel, conduit or connection, which is <u>Alpha Spirit</u> "Awareness" as Spiritual Life or ZU. The Alpha Spirit engages a <u>ZU-line</u>, a spiritual life-line of ZU energy to a genetic vehicle or organic body to experience physical beta existence.

MARDUKITE ZUISM DEFINITIONS FOR SYSTEMOLOGY.

<u>ALPHA SPIRIT</u> = a spiritual lifeform; the True Self or "I-AM"; the spirit that is controlling the physical body or "genetic vehicle" using a Lifeline or continuum of spiritual "ZU" energy.

<u>ASCENSION</u> = actualized Awareness elevated to (AN) spiritual existence that is exterior to beta-existence.

BETA-EXISTENCE = manifestation in the Physical Universe (KI); the state of existence or condition of frequency specific to physical energy and physical matter in physical space.

FRAGMENTATION = breaking into parts; fractioning wholeness; fracture of holism; discontinuity; separation; outside the state of Self-Honesty.

GENETIC VEHICLE = a physical lifeform; the physical (beta) body controlled by the (Alpha) Spirit using a continuous Lifeline of ZU energy.

HUMAN CONDITION = a default programmed conditioned state standard issue Human existence/experience.

ZU-LINE = a spectrum of Spiritual Life-Energy (ZU); an energetic channel or Identity-Continuum connecting Alpha Spirit Awareness from Infinity-to-Infinity including the full physical beta range.

THE HIGHEST FORM OF
TRUE DIVINE WORSHIP.

The true Destiny of Humanity is to achieve spiritual <u>Self-Actualization</u>; the reunion of Self with the Divine. Attaining Self-Honesty in this Life is the most important step a person can take toward achieving their highest ideals, goals and realizations.

The Highest form of "True Worship" begins with the Spirit—the true Self—and all external practices, rituals, ceremonies and historical examples are but outer reflections of this ideal. The Highest form of "Sin" is against the Spirit —against the Self—and its ability to maintain Self-Honesty. There are modes of thought, action and Self-direction of effort that will contribute toward Ascension; and modes that lead away from that.

Beta experiences of "Sin"—pain, fear, guilt, anger—are all related to personal fragmentation; and emotional turbulence from all of these may be released—and intention energy redirected— because: <u>we are all co-creators of Reality in this lifetime!</u>

SPHERES OF EXISTENCE, INFLUENCE & UTILITARIAN ETHICS OF SYSTEMOLOGY.

The prime directive of all beta existence is: *to exist*. The continuation of existence is the purpose behind all existence. Between realization of Self and Infinity, there are many spheres of existence that we may influence. All of the spheres are interconnected.

There is nothing in existence that is in absolute exclusion to all existence. Each sphere of existence supports subsequent existences and assists reaches toward higher spheres of influence.

The greatest good contributes to the greatest continuation of optimum existence for the greatest sphere of inclusion. Degrees of rightness and wrongness are determined by Cosmic Law and are reflected in the quality of, and continuation of, an optimal existence at the highest sphere of existence.

Individual happiness is attained via the channel to the highest sphere. Human unhappiness is the result of "selfishness" and/or lack of "spiritual Self-Actualization" and "Awareness."

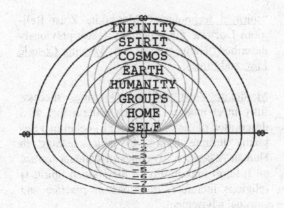

ZU : MARDUKITE ZUISM & MODERN ZUIST RELIGION.

History demonstrates how dangerous, trouble-some and easily misused the concept of "REL-GION" is; so, for purposes of incorporating Mardukite Zuism as a contemporary standard, the idea of "religion" is here treated as:

a concise spiritual paradigm, set of be-liefs and practices, regarding Divinity, Infinite Beingness—or else "God."

<u>Mardukite Zuism</u> operates under a premise of very specific beliefs and a "<u>systemology</u>" of

"spiritual technology." Mardukite Zuist Religious Doctrine fundamentally relays previously described "Highest forms" of Worship, Cosmic Law, and Ethics.

Mardukite Zuist Spiritual Doctrines successfully meet modern religious criteria for: a) a description of cosmic creation; b) belief in a Supreme Infinite Being; c) ethics leading to Human Ascension; d) ethics of conduct toward all Life; e) Immortality of the Human Spirit; f) religious literature, traditions of practice and spiritual advisement.

GOALS & IDEALS OF MARDUKITE ZUISM.

The word "ZU" meant "knowing" in original Sumerian cuneiform script. Goals and ideals of Zuism reflect this. Mardukite Zuism seeks to assist an individual in reclaiming a realization of the True Self or "I-AM" as the Immortal Spirit, in line with a most ancient directive: to "Know Thyself."

In view of the fact that all modern humans are subjected to technologies depriving them of their freedoms to *be*, *think*, *know* and pursue truth: the goals and ideals of Zuism are to effectively revive and repair these very abilities and certainties of the Individual—as an increase of "Actualized Awareness."

INFINITY, "GOD" & SUPREME BEINGNESS

The Spiritual Philosophy of Zuism is systematized by a Standard Model. It demonstrates Absolute Supreme Beingness associated with the Highest realization of "God" as INFINITY. No thing is Higher or Absolute than the Infinity of Nothing—and reducing Supreme Beingness to any finite personality or character trait is to limit and defile with lesser "words."

The Highest Name of God cannot be conceived —hence our symbolic use of the Infinity Sign:

∞

...or Sumerian cuneiform word-sign: "ABZU" —"The Infinite Nothingness and Source of All ZU."

The Spiritual Universe (AN) is *All-as-One* because it exists as an infinite singularity or stasis:

infinite potential with no gradient or observed motion; which is its own continuity.

The Physical Universe (KI) is *All-as-One* because it is in continuous motion, with all manifest parts working systematically as a continuity of beta-existence.

A "spiritual continuum" or "conduit channel" of ZU—absolute energy from the Spiritual Universe (AN)—links our Awareness levels of "I-AM," "True Self" or Spirit ("Alpha Spirit") with the degrees of motion and variation in the Physical Universe.

This Alpha Spirit or "Soul" is the true Awareness, "I" or "Self" connected to the operation and control of the physical body.

THE TRUE HUMAN ALPHA SPIRIT.

The true Self is the "I" or "Spirit" regardless of its position, degree or level of Awareness. Spirit remains. Whatever "spiritual energy-matter" composes the Alpha Spirit or "soul"—it must occupy this "other space" with its spiritual existence and then project its Awareness and Will onto the Physical Universe (KI) in order to experience the Game we call Life.

This "spiritual energy-matter" that composes all Life (as a Lifeforce with Awareness and Consciousness) goes by many names throughout history—but we find the idea first treated as <u>ZU</u> on cuneiform tablets of Mesopotamia.

On an Identity lifeline of ZU energy, all Alpha Spirits are operating from a Spiritual Universe. We refer to this as the ZU-line on the Standard Model.

ZU is the name given to the spiritual essence of all Life in existence—and Self is a concentrated center or focal point as a ZU-continuum or Identity.

The True Self of an Individual Human is a "spiritual universe cause" of "physical universe effects"—engaging as an immortal Alpha Spirit with a Self-determined Will actualized as an Awareness along the ZU-continuum, extending from Infinity-to-Infinity, through every possible frequency and vibration along the total spectrum of physical and metaphysical existence.

THE SYSTEMOLOGY PRACTICES OF SPIRITUAL ADVISEMENT & COUNSELING SERVICES FOR MARDUKITE ZUISM.

The Mardukite Chamberlains were established in 2009 dedicated to recovery and consolidation of all historical, scriptural & ritual records of ancient Babylon in Mesopotamia. In 2011, a Mardukite faction (International Systemology Society) began to research and develop methods to apply ancient wisdom as a futurist spiritual technology that awakens, unlocks and fully actualizes spiritual potential of the Human Condition.

A systematic approach to spirituality is seen on the Standard Model, where ZU-line frequencies are represented at various degrees: "zero-point" body death; cellular activity and sensory perceptions of a genetic body; bio-chemicals induced by emotion; thoughts and intention transmitted between our Alpha Spirit and the "genetic vehicle"—all the way "up" the scale to a perfected clarity of Self-Actualized Awareness of I-AM as our true "Alpha" state, just below Infinity and Absolute Beingness. Full potential of ZU in Consciousness is only altered from its natural state as a result of personal fragmentation of the Human Condition. This may be restored with spiritual practices.

The Pathway to Self-Honesty is a personal journey and spiritual adventure marked by progressive clearing of spiritual energy channels fragmented by the imprinting and programming accumulated from experiences in our environment—the "debris" that fragments the total actualized experience of Self in Awareness as the Alpha Spirit.

The first and most important step—Before an individual can actualize potentials of the Spirit as Self, they must fully realize: the I-AM Self and the Alpha Spirit are One.

This state of Knowingness is the primary intention of basic spiritual practices found in Mardukite Zuism.

"Systemology" books and advanced training courses are also available to Mardukite Ministers seeking to qualify as specialized clergy, priests, priestess, and systematic processing pilots.

CREED OF MARDUKITE ZUISM.
PRINCIPLES OF BELIEF.[*]

1.) We believe in an Absolute Beingness, which is Infinite—the ABZU—the All-as-One encompassing Source of All Being, Knowing and Awareness to all Alpha (Spiritual-AN) and Beta (Physical-KI) states of existence.

2.) We believe in a spiritual energy of all Life and Awareness—ZU—in the physical universe (beta) that is an effect of a spiritual (Alpha) cause; a Spirit that is cause. This Spirit—in its Alpha state—is the True Self "I-AM" Individual Identity that many have called the "soul."

3.) We believe that the Human Condition is a genetic vehicle used by a spiritual source (AN) to experience the Finite as physical existence (KI)—that we are Awareness (ZU) projected onto a genetic vehicle—and that while the vehicle/body may perish to physical entropy, the "Alpha Spirit" remains immortal and Self-directed to the extent of its own Actualized Awareness.

---

[*] First drafted in 2019.

4.) We believe that the highest form of worship and spirituality is the actualization and advancement of our "Self" as Spirit in Self-Honesty—and that Self-Honesty is the I-AM Alpha state of Being and Knowing, which is realizable in this lifetime.

5.) We believe that the purpose of all existence is: to exist—and that the prime directive of all spiritual Life is: continued existence of spiritual Life and co-creation of habitable Reality. "Good" and "Moral" actions are evaluated to the extent of this end.

6A.) We believe that no Life exists in exclusion to all other Life—and that the conditions of a habitable Reality extending from Self include:
Home; Community; All Humanity; All Life on Earth; All Life in the Universe; All Spiritual Life; and the Infinite.

6B.) We believe in a continued evolution of Alpha Spirit awareness developed beyond one physical life, and that a Spirit experiences many.

7A.) We believe Mardukite Zuism and its applied systemology is a 21st Century AD synthesis of the 21st Century BC wisdom collected on cuneiform tablets and experienced in ancient Mesopotamia, esp. Babylon.

7B.) This cuneiform library included details concerning: beings called the Anunnaki; ordering of the Cosmos; creation of Humanity; and an entire legacy of systematized traditions.

8.) We believe in the continuation of, and proper communication of, the true legacy of Human history—and the ability of every Human to realize that they are a Free Spirit in a Free Zone of Self-Determinism: and no "evils" can affect intentions if an individual is spiritually Self-Actualized in Self-Honesty.

THE ARCANE KNOWLEDGE FROM MARDUK'S TABLET OF DESTINY.[*]

1.) As above, so below;
On earth as it is in Heaven
an-bala ki-bala an-ba ki an-ba

2.) What the Mind believes, the Spirit reinforces
da-ga nam-ku-zu dingir-Lamma a bi-ib-gar

3.) When disaster is self-made,
no man can interfere
*nig-ku-lam-ma dingir-ra-na-ka su—
tu-tu nu-ub-zu*

4.) What is given in submission
is a catalyst for defiance
nig-gu-gar-ra nig-gaba-gar-ra

5.) Whoever partners with Truth, creates Life
nig-ge-na-ta a-ba in-da-di nam-ti i-u-tu

---

[*] Excerpted from *"Tablets of Destiny"* by Joshua Free.

THE SUMERIAN

ANUNNAKI

MARDUKITE LIBER-50

*In the Beginning
was an
Infinity of
Nothingness...*

— 00 —

ABZU : THE PRIMORDIAL ABYSS

For some, it is far too esoteric to say—the true and actual nature of all existence is an "Infinity of Nothingness." Yet, the most ancient spiritual texts suggest this is so. One may even believe they understand the meaning of the very words *"infinity"* and *"nothingness"*—but there is no guarantee this has been properly relayed in the past. Mysterious lore of the *Abyss* is reflected in mystical accounts from around the globe, spanning the entire evolution of human civilization.

A true understanding of this critical state is paramount to real "mystical" work—what is hidden at the heart of most ancient esoteric spirituality. Secrets of the *Ancient Mystery School* affected all systematized living, including the Sumerians. These "secrets" evolved, giving way to later Chaldeo-Babylonian "systems"—forms of "mysticism" and, dare we call it, "magic." Today, we see renewed interest in these matters among both academic scholars and those in the contemporary New Age. But, since the philosophies of the "Classical" era, shamanic cultures of Europe, or even the Egyptians all seem more "accessible" to the modern *"seeker,"* the deeper and more ancient mysteries of Mesopotamia seem to often fade into shadows.

Outside of the original esoteric sects, imaginations of the uninitiated surged passed their historical understanding, and a plethora of traditions and systems diverted from the main well-springs, continuing to deflect consciousness further from truly understanding primordial origins.

On the "Arcane Tablets," the *Primordial Abyss* was originally nameless—an "Infinity of Nothingness." As the latent, unmanifest, potentiality of *"Everythingness,"* the *Abyss* is the "All-Source" for any manifestation of *things* in material existence. This concept was not only abstract to the ancients, it remains in the realm of *esoterica* today.

To compensate for a lack of *exoteric* public understanding, "pantheist" philosophers arose to equate universal forces with more tangible concepts—physical places names for beings or "creatures." Originally used to philosophically illustrate examples, such beings and places were *so closely* identified with otherwise esoteric concepts in the minds of the general population, that they were blatantly assimilated in consciousness and mythology as direct embodiments of these cosmic forces or principles.

Cuneiform tablets from the priest-scribes of *Nabu* also provide evidence for an ancient belief in an "All-Encompassing Being" *begotten* of "the Abyss and the Primordial Sea." This means the *true infinity* of "nothingness" or what we might call "zero" is actually an *a priori* unity of "infinite aspects of itself" as all possible aetheric space—the "nothingness" and the "spaces between" as "One," "All," or rather, "None." This "formula" is generally represented as "*zero times zero*" or "OO"—the *sign of Infinity*. To quote the English philosopher, George Henry Lewes—If zero "0" is the sign of vanished quantity, then the Infinite "00" is the sign of total continuity.

Fundamentally, the beauty and simplicity of the infinitude of space and pure potentiality of existence is enough for an "All-Encompassing Being," but this is an almost "static" existence with no forces in movement—quite simply All-is-One (*or none!*) in the universe. This background non-existence is not animated—not manifest—and so requires "motion" for any existence. This was born of duality, but of the highest spiritual intent and not to be confused with some mundane spiritual morality. For it was only by the opposition of the primordial currents of "chaos" and "order"—"No-Thing" and "All-Things"—that the cosmos were causally set in motion with a pendulum-like drive toward constant activity, progression and "*unfoldment*" that we call "existence."

The "unrest" of forces is a necessary condition for "Cosmic Law," "The All" or "One" to exist; fragmented by its very first division—that of "exist-ence" and "naught"—the *first dichotomy*.

The *pure potentiality* of "infinite shape, form and variety, in all time, space and quantity" was diffi-cult to relay in primitive language. However, esoteric interpretation of the most ancient Sumeri-an semantics of an "All-Being" is best reflected by the original meaning of the word "ILU" in Chaldeo-Babylonian literature. The original conce-pt appeared in Sumerian language as "DIN.GIR," meaning "All-God," but later cultural pantheistic interpretations applied this term to individual per-sonified "gods." The "Babylon" city, nation and culture was actually named in honor of their own spiritual quest—a "re-connection" with this *"Source"* by "ascending" the "Ladder of Lights" or "BAB.ILU"—The Gateway to God, or original "Tower of Babel."

True esoteric meaning was lost in time as the word was equated with "gods." An evolving Mesopot-amian language system also associated it to "stars," almost changing the function of *Babylon* in consciousness as the "Doorway to the Stars," or as fictional character Daniel Jackson would prefer, a "Star-Gate." Original symbolism and simplicity of the truth is immediately shattered when enters philosophers, scholars and religious scientists—for we have all-too-easily overlooked a stumbling block when interpreting the most ancient tablets

concerning divinity. As Lenormant explains in
Chaldean Magic & Sorcery:—

> "[For] the idea of ILU was too compre-
> hensive and too vast to receive a very
> definite exterior form, and consequently
> [too obscure for] the adoration of the
> people. The personality of ILU was not
> clearly defined for a long time; his office
> and title as "God One" were at first given
> to Anu, "the ancient god," and the first per-
> son of the supreme trinity, which was
> afterward held to emanate from ILU; the
> priests did not distinguish the primordial
> principle from the chief of this trinity."

It is here, from the start of our discourse on
"Sumerian Religion," that a true *Seeker* should
learn to differentiate the "pantheistic personalities"
of cultural mythology from the raw esoteric representations. When we exclusively focus on
outward expressions of relative stories and histor-
ies, any deeper esoteric truths are shroud in
mystery and lost to interpretation. If we were to
base our cosmogony on purely Chaldeo-Babylonian accounts, one might be led to assume that Anu
is born from ILU directly, and then in many regards becomes one and the same as ILU.
Mythological "Order" of the *cosmos* is entrusted
to the Sumerian "All-Father" of the *Anunnaki gods*
as an embodiment of the same. But, physically and

literally, Sumerian tablets do not actually ascribe Anu the position of *a priori* "First Being."

Sumerian mythology is troublesome when concerning names, since many titles can be shared by a single being, and what's worse, these titles often get exchanged between various beings at different times and by different tablet authors. At least three sets of "Divine Union" are found to precede the existence of Anu on many of the Sumerian tablets. These names are transliterated by early Sumeriologists as: ABZU and TIAMAT; MUMMU and LAKMU (or LAHMU and LAHAMU); and, ANSAR and KISAR.

The first pair of names are the most applicable to our current chapter—titles with attributes traditionally associated with the *"Abyss"* (ABZU) and the *"Primordial Sea"* (TIAMAT), which as One, compose "nothingness" and "everythingness." Some interpretations confuse these two principles as the same, but they are not. Where the *Abyss* is an infinity of unmanifest potential, the *primordial sea* is an infinity or recursive continuum of form—the *First Cause*—or the "Law" put in motion as infinite manifestation. [The later "Divine Couples" are intended to represent this "2=0" creative principle of "Order" in the *cosmos*.]

Biblical scholars now have conceded to the idea that the Semitic books, like *Genesis*, are indeed the product of a far more ancient Mesopotamian literary influence "God," the creator of existence, is found alone and everywhere at once, a "*primordial sea*" washing through an "*infinite abyss*." Samuel Kramer summarizes in his *Sumerian Mythology*:—

> "*First was the primeval sea.* Nothing concerning the origin or creation of the primeval sea has as yet been discovered in the available Sumerian texts, and the indications are that the Sumerian sages looked upon the primeval sea as a kind of first cause and prime mover."

In the Babylonian *Enuma Elis* "Epic of Creation," ABZU (or APSU) is the first name given, and to it the trait of "primeval," or else the "one who was from the beginning." This persona is later passed on to the local sun by later philosophers and mythographers. In the rendering of this *Epic* on *Tablet-N* with our Mardukite "Anunnaki Bible," we read:

> *And the primeval APZU, who birthed them,*
> *And CHAOS—TIAMAT, the Ancient One,*
> *Mother to them all.*

And from a bastardized version in Simon's *Necronomicon*:—

> *And naught existed but the Seas of ABZU,*
> *the Ancient One,*

And MUMMU TIAMAT,
the Ancient One, who bore them all.

Where TIAMAT is listed with ABZU ("*and their waters were as one*"), MUMMU is introduced to us in some versions as a "counselor" or "vizier"— a messenger for the pair. The "Epic" continues, informing us that that the other "Divine Couples" were called into being and/or created. Yet, on some other tablets, the word MUMMU or NAMMU is attributed to an *Anunnaki goddess*, a "pantheistic personification" of a humanoid deity synonymous with abstract cosmic role of TIAMAT. Kramer goes on to illustrate this:—

> "The goddess *Nammu*, written with the ideogram for 'sea' is described as 'the life-mother, who gave birth to heaven and earth' [*ti-ama-tu-an-ki*] (or *ama-palil-u-tu-dingir-sar-sar-ra-ke-ne*, 'the mother, the ancestress who have birth to all the gods'). Heaven and Earth were therefore conceived by the Sumerians as the created products of the primeval sea."

Opening lines of the "*Epic of Creation*" confirm these beings existed "*before the heavens and earth were named,*" meaning before material existence were divided into an ordered existence—for in the beginning was All-as-One, and even in the first creative expression, "*their waters were as one.*"

The first progression or motion of the creative force was to manifest its "every-thing-ness" and "no-thing-ness"—the all-encompassing universe— distinguished on cuneiform tablets by uniting the most basic Sumerian words for "heaven" and "earth," or else, AN and KI. Literally: "heaven-earth," the ancient Sumerians understood AN-KI to mean "universe"—the entirety of the *cosmos,* both "seen" and "unseen."

These powers are called forth to bare witness and offer aid to every magical charm and prayer of Mesopotamian religion:—

> *Spirit of the Heavens, Remember!*
> *Spirit of the Earth, Remember!*

— 0 —

TIAMAT : THE PRIMEVAL DRAGON

The first creature spawned from out of the abyss—
the *Cosmic Dragon*—to whom the Sumerians
would give no less a title than: "Mother of All Creation." In Hebrew, the word is "*tehom*," meaning
"the deep" or "primordial sea," by which this force
receives recognition in the Semitic *Genesis*. In an
infinite universe not yet manifest, the "*primeval
dragon*"—TIAMAT—is the "*first cause*" made by
the Absolute, the first fragmentation from wholeness and oneness into existence—the "Law of
ALL" put in motion.

In most ancient mythology, the *primeval dragon* is
personified as the "Mother of All Creation." This
force, identifiably female, is credited with creation
of the other "*gods*," including all corporeal spirits
visible on earth in ancient times as the "*Anunnaki*." This belief found its way into modern "New
Age" theories explaining physical aspects of the
gods as "reptilian" in nature, descended from a
"Great Cosmic Dragon." By definition, all existences fall under this "*Cosmic Law*"—all existences are extensions of the same "*Universal
Agent*."

The essence of wholeness (or duality in wholeness) is represented in the Mesopotamian pantheon
as "divine unions" or couples. Both the male and

female aspects are seen as reflections of as one—though like the physical sexes manifest of man, they are divided for our interpretation as being "god" and "goddess." Depending on the tablet sources, the deeds and attributes of one are often placed on the other, demonstrating that the full qualities are complete only when paired. For this reason, early scholars examining the Creation tablets mistook ABZU (*the Abyss*) as literal "consort" of TIAMAT. But after *his* "death," in the Babylonian account, her husband-partner is listed as KINGU.

Let us be clear, however, that more than ABZU, KINGU or any other primordial name listed on pre-Anunnaki lists of "rulership" in heaven, it is the *primeval dragon*—called "TIAMAT"—that is attributed all active ability of creation in the Universe.

As the primal force or "prime mover" of a physical existence that came out of the *Abyss*, our first "deity" (if we are to call it such) is not only a dragon, but female, and her consort is given the more passive role for the act of creation. Under the epitaph of "*Nammu*," "*Mammu*," "*Mummu*," "*Mammi*" or "*Mami*" (of which was later assimilated into the Babylonian goddess *Aruru*, among others), she is the "Creator Goddess" and "Mother of All Mortal Life," offering up her blood (or "sand from her beaches") to be mixed with the

"*Breath of Enlil*" and "*Waters of Enki*" for the creation of human life on earth.

The "name" of MUMMU is actually evoked in Babylonian magic—the "*Grimoire of Marduk*" or "Book of Fifty Names"—derived from the seventh tablet of the *Enuma Elis*. The thirty-fourth name listed is "MUMMU," who as we have said, is sometimes confused with TIAMAT, but is instead her "vizier" or "chief-minister"—the "active messenger principle." From the "Mardukite" perspective, all aspects of the Fifty Names are attributed to the power of *Marduk* in Babylon:—

> "...the power given to *Marduk* to fashion the universe from the flesh of TIAMAT offers wisdom concerning the condition of life before the creation, and nature of the structures of the Four Pillars whereupon the Heavens rest."

This active principle—MUMMU—is described both as the "Creator of the Universe" and also the "Guardian to the Gate to the Outside," but is not originally a "power" of *Marduk*, by Sumerian standards. Based on what we know concerning Babylonian adaptations of earlier Sumerian literature, the "Fifty Names" adopted by *Marduk* in their tradition were really names of the fifty preexisting "*Anunnaki gods*," some of which are actually mentioned in the *Enuma Elis*, playing active roles during the infamous "war in heaven." It is equally possible, on a cosmological level, that these names reflect some fifty "primary elements" composing the *cosmos* at its material inception. The Babylonian *"Epic"* describes the turbulent formation of earth and humans from "star-stuff" using symbolism of a violent battle between Marduk and TIAMAT. Michanowsky queries in *"Once and Future Star"*:—

> "The great riddle is why the primordial sea, which according to Sumerian belief, brought forth the world around us without conflict or confrontation, had suddenly been recast [in Chaldeo-Babylonian literature] in the image of a vicious demon mother who had to be denounced as a menace to law and order and then cruelly destroyed."

With the rise of later generations of gods, a theme of unseating or dethroning the positions of the original and most ancient pantheon took hold. This dualistic viewpoint is most obvious during the Babylonian era, including later Assyrian offshoots.

We see the first militant acknowledgment of a generational gap between the "younger" and "elder" pantheons in the *"Enuma Elis,"* where the "elders" are either demonized as "evil," removed from the system entirely, or given only passing mention. Compared to earlier Sumerian beliefs, this dualism would seem artificial, created for the sole purpose of elevating the position of the younger pantheon, observed in Babylon, as the supreme forces in the local universe and thereby usurping their ancestors. What could not be done physically was accomplished in a manner that ruling classes have used since the dawn of history: the very *alteration* of said *history*.

Lore of this rebellion is found in post-Sumerian religious and mystical doctrines that identify with a "good versus evil" motif. We see it in the foundations of nearly all later traditions. From Babylon it spread east to Persia and west to Egypt, where its oldest forms are drawn as antagonistic moral dogmas held by Chaldeo-Babylonians, Egyptians and Zoroastrians. The Semitic traditions also inherited this "dualism," as reflected today in contemporary forms of Islam, Judaism and Christianity—all of which are strongly rooted in opposition and polar worldviews. This is found nowhere in ancient Sumer and seems to attach itself later on to the *Primeval Dragon* icon. It is, perhaps, only loosely based on the "Destruction of KUR," understood by modern Sumeriologists only in relation to other known pantheons, as Kramer does:—

> "...the monstrous creature which at least in a certain sense corresponds to the Babylonian goddess Tiamat, the Hebrew Leviathan and perhaps the Greek Typhon."

In more widely known versions of the Babylonian "*Epic of Creation*" [translated fully in this antholgy as *Tablet-N* and *Tablet-F*] we are given an amazing account of how the patron of Babylon— *Marduk*—fights and destroys an "evil dragon," TIAMAT. We are spared no gruesome details of the bloody massacre awaiting her, finalized by an execution-styled beheading. We can see parallels of "*god-kings*" rivaling Chaos-Dragons in many later mythologies. However, on the most ancient tablets of Mesopotamia, this is a dramatic "cosmo-logical" event. After TIAMAT is slain, half of her ("the head") is used to create the "*heavens*" ("AN") and the other half ("the body") is used to create the "*earth*" ("KI")—or, "AN-KI," the mani-fested universe. Some "astrophysical" interpreta-tions of these tablets inspire belief that the epic de-scribes a "collision theory" for the local solar sys-tem, particularly concerning formation of earth and moon.

We must assume that the philosophical minds that so carefully devised the Chaldeo-Babylonian sys-tem (which became so important for the Egyptians and other mystical and Semitic cultures) never fathomed that the tablets of their Sumerian ancest-ors, sometimes predating them by thousands of years, would ever be recovered. I

t seemed that for a time, evidence for Sumerian civilization did disappear from human consciousness, replaced instead by the *Genesis* offered by Babylonians and later derived Semitic lore. In fact, they were using the same written writing system, the same pantheon, and many of the same cosmological concepts under varying guises. "Superimposition" at a literary level appeared seamless.

It was not until the late 1800's that "Assyriologists" realized that some of the tablets and artifacts excavated from the Middle East were pre-Semitic —from before the *Akkadians*. It is now clear that "proper" formation and order of the primordial universe was adjusted to meet political and spiritual needs of a tribal people rapidly turned metropolitan, raising the position of their local deity to support the famous and widespread influence of *Babylon*.

It is understood then that the "Elder Gods" or "Ancient Ones" are overridden by the "younger gods"—those most most accessible in all global mythologies, usually representing planets of the local solar system in every instance. By "associating" themselves with visible "Celestial Spheres" in the sky, the Anunnaki install themselves as a staple at the origins of modern Human civilization.

Putting the physical cosmology of ABZU and TIAMAT aside—as the *Infinity of Nothing* and the *Prime Cause*—the emphasis of the current discourse is primarily on the pantheistic applications

to Sumerian *Anunnaki* lore. It is difficult to determine if this "War in Heaven" among sentient
"*gods*" did actually take place or if it was only
written about later as propaganda to blot out the
significance and contribution of their ancestors.
Although not necessarily a moral facet, TIAMAT
directly represents the *first existence*—the first
separation of wholeness from the All-Source. This,
in itself, generates a belief for many, in a "fall
from grace" or "removal from the Source"—what
is really at the heart of all dualism in global religions. This is most obvious in Gnostic lore—
which views all physical existence as "evil," contrast to purely non-material "Godly" or spiritual
existence.

If realizing that we occupy physical bodies in separation, removed from "God" directly, we can
understand how the human psyche might demon-
ize the form "first removed" as the cause of our
own fragmentation. Our ability in explaining this
awareness on various "levels" in no way condones
behaviors of the younger generation of *gods*. But
they too, must have experienced the same philo-
sophic and spiritual devastation of this realization
—and at an understandably higher degree of comprehension.

Dualistic conflict of "forces" in the universe are a
necessary property of its existence in movement,
but it is not necessarily subject to the "moral dual-

ism" that humans identify with. Forces are constantly working with and against once another to keep "the organized universe" the way it is—and continually moving to the way it will be. Without this, there is only the static and "Infinite Nothing" existence of the original state of ALL, which we cannot even inhabit and still be separated as a being of *Self*. Thus, the real "division" is essentially what is visible and what is not visible (from "human" perspective)—for the infinitude we inhabit contains everything and nothing can not exist. In Sumerian mythology, this is observed in the union or bond of "heaven-earth" (AN-KI) as a singular aspect; as a dual aspect, the seen and unseen aspects of reality; and as a zero aspect, still encompassed in and of the abyssal nothingness. Sumerians depicted this abstract form as a "*mountain*," the physical "bond" between "heaven" and "earth." *Ziggurats* were built as a reflection of the same.

We have previously mentioned the "Destruction of KUR" in passing. Not only does the word KUR mean "mountain," but it appears in the only significant "dragon-slaying" example from pre-Mardukite Sumerian literature. This time, however, KUR is not a cthonic abyssal water-based dragon, but is instead deep in the earth, in the mountain—or in a very literal sense, the mountain (earth) itself. There are three available Sumerian versions of this tablet cycle, each successively more recent in its origination, as the characters change. Kramer conveniently paraphrases the three versions:—

> "The first involves the water-god Enki, whose closest parallel among the Greeks is Poseidon. The hero of the second is Ninurta, the prototype for the Babylon god Marduk when playing the role of 'hero of the gods' in the Babylonian Epic of Creation. In the third, Inanna, counterpart of the Semitic Ishtar, plays the leading role. In all three versions, however, the monster being destroyed is termed KUR."

KUR is an obscure enigma for the prehistoric Sumerian pantheistic worldview, which is otherwise orderly and peaceful. Only later with increased human population did disharmony arise, wrought by new traditions of "evil sorcerers" commanding chaotic "demons" of plague and pestilence. But these expressions are merely accelerated entropy in motion—the opposite of growth and nurture. They do not seem to correlate with a dualistic nature of "good versus evil" applied to our lore of the archetypal primeval dragon. This force only appears chaotic due to its infinite expressions of "change" and "birth"—like the amoral explosive emission of life from seed or egg.

Some esoteric texts render TIAMAT as the "Ancient of Days." In the Chaldeo-Babylonian kabbalistic system—also called the *Ladder of Lights*—a mystic confronts TIAMAT ladder as the "Dweller on the Threshold" or "Guardian of the Gate to the Outside"—as a representation of the "Fear of the Unknown" that blocks progress. In other traditions of magic, it is KHORONZON, the "Dragon of Chaos" encountered in the dimensional ascent of astral pathwork.

Modern mystical encounters with this energy may prove challenging for some who hold onto the more animated depictions of a primeval "Dragon of Chaos." This current of power is rather subtle (or gentle) like the waves of the sea, but they can just as easily turn turbulent when perturbed. Anthropomorphic manifestations and astral encounters with a personification of TIAMAT generally reflect her "reptilian" form as a sleek black dragon. Rarely she may assume a more human form, almost resembling Semitic lore of "*Lilith,*" but always female, and usually with black hair. In *Babylon*, The Tiamat Gate is essentially the "*Gate to the Outside,*" which is to say in more esoterically acceptable terms, the "*Gate to the Abyss.*"

— I —

ANU : KINGSHIP IN HEAVEN

Literature from the Sumerian tradition—cuneiform tablets unearthed during the last century—reveals that the Anunnaki system is the original archetypal "Olympian" pantheon of deities copied and pasted onto diverse cultures for thousands of years.

The Anunnaki were originally assigned to twelve positions in the cosmos forming a celestial sphere around the earth (later yielding lore of the "zodiac") and to twelve bodies of our local solar system (ten planets, plus the sun and moon). Prior to the "Ammonite" fascination with the local Sun, best observed among the Egyptians and other solar-cults, it was this collective star-system (or "pantheon") that the ancients deemed the "Rulers of Fate" and "Keepers of the Sacred Cycles on Earth"—the cosmic order of the organized universe.

"Ancient Ones" from Sumerian prehistory— ABZU, TIAMAT, LAHAMU, &tc.—are given brief mention in cuneiform literature, but are viewed as more abstract or metaphysical properties of creation, not accessibly appropriate as traditional deities. We have shown in other chapters how such forces could be seen as the primordial essence of the "All-Source" being first made manifest. But the Sumerians also viewed these act-

ive properties as materializing in their own personified "All-Father"—*Anu*—a figurehead for the
hierarchical pantheon. These traits or energetic
currents of primordial forces are assimilated by
successively "younger gods" as they are elevated
to higher roles in the hierarchy.

The genealogy given in the *Enuma Elis* "Epic of
Creation" depicts ANSAR (or *Anshar*) and KISAR
(*Kishar*) as father and mother of AN ("*Anu*" in
Chaldeo-Babylonian). It is *Anu*, in turn, that is
credited as "Father" of both the I.GI.GI—a legion
of "celestial spirits" who "watch" and "see"—and
the AN.UN.NA.KI (or Anunna-Ki, sometimes
spelled "Anunna-Ge" by early Sumeriologists)—
or else a pantheon of "gods" who *decree the fates
of earth.*" It is Zecharia Sitchin that put forth the
more commonly known translation of "*heaven
down to earth.*"

The names ANSAR and KISAR are most coherently translated as "heaven-zone" and "earth-
zone" respectively. "SAR" means "cycle" or "the
round of" in *Babylonian* language. If we adhere to
this defined cosmology, their division as separate
and then unity as wholeness is the progenitive
spark producing an archetypal lineage of distinct
and sentient gods born directly from the "omni-di-
mension," first known to itself only as the Abyss,
then separated by the Primordial Waters and then
finally condensed and separated as "heaven" and

"earth." Some folk have put forth the suggestion that the *Anunnaki* actually entered our earthly "time-space" from another dimension or star-system.

Most cuneiform tablets are written very "matter-of-factly," almost reminiscent of "technical writing." Their authors felt no need to "validate" or "prove" an existence of the *Anunnaki* any further—just as we today write our events and history as "statements" that are fundamentally understood within the context of our culture. Naturally, the oldest surviving Sumerian accounts of the "creation of the universe" are sparse and badly fractured. References to AN ("*Anu*") specifically, are few in number when compared to his later and more active children. While the actually name and power is frequently called upon, very few tablets are dedicated to *Anu* specifically. Rather than petitions for aid, they are often "hymns" of praise, as reflected in this seven-line cuneiform tablet fragment, translated by L.W. King:—

1. *siptu bilu sur-bu-[u]*... "Mighty Lord..."
2. *ilu-Anim sur-bu-[u]*... "Anu, Mighty Lord..."
3. *ilu sami-i*... "God of the Sky..."
4. *ilu-Anim ilu sami-[i]*... "Anu, god of the Sky..."
5. *pa-sir u-mi*... "Loosener of the Day..."

6. *ilu-Anim pa-[sir u-mi]...* "Anu, Loosener
of Day..."
7. *pa-sir sunati...* "Interpreter of Dreams..."

As we see in more popular interpretations from the last century, academic scholars have filled in many cracks of these broken tablets with the lore presented in post-Sumerian periods. The farther away from the original simplicity of the tradition that we get, however, the more strongly the Semitic influences and those of Zoroastrian dualism are incorporated. Again, academicians have often employed the reverse engineering method of working backwards from more familiar (and relatively more recent) systems in which to interpret antiquated and more obscure ones. This is purely fallacious, especially given what we commonly know regarding the degradation of information transmission (communication) over time.

It is sometimes difficult to separate the interpretation of Anu's position without conjuring up lore connected to his offspring. Many tablet authors began their sagas and incantations with some kind of unifying genesis to support why such and such happened or where such a such draws their power from, like the following, Kramer translates:—

*After heaven had been moved away from
the earth,
After earth had been separated from the*

> *heavens,*
> *After the name of man had been fixed;*
> *After AN had carried off heaven,*
> *After Enlil had carried off earth,*
> *After Ereshkigal had been carried off into*
> *KUR as its prize...*

Following sequential logic of the above passage, unity of creation fractured into dual existence of "heaven" and "earth," which were then separated from one another. In this ancient Sumerian version, AN "carries" off heaven, becoming responsible for the organization and order of heaven, and his son *Enlil* is left to oversee work concerning physical existence on Earth. [And in this instance, "KUR" is used synonymously as *"Underworld."*]

Later Assyrio-Babylonian or *"Mardukite"* versions attribute more of these responsibilities to the lineage of Anu's *other* son, *Enki* (or EA) and his son, *Marduk*—figures receiving little attention in the purely Sumerian sources, also for political reasons.

The position of Anu in the Sumerian pantheon is as an undisputed *"Father in Heaven,"* who acts as the supreme "progenitor" or "father of the gods" from his place as the "King of the Local Universe." The *"House of Anu"* (the traditional "heaven" or "abode of the gods") is sometimes written as UR.ANU or *"Uranus"* (from the Greek *"Ouranos"*). His most sacred place of "worship" on earth was in the city of Uruk at the temple of E.ANNA—also translated to mean "*House of Anu.*" The number of his rank is sixty—the number of cosmic perfection, or "whole value," in Mesopotamian mathematics—similar to our "100," but expressed in their entire mathematical system in a manner similar to our own retention of their division of a *whole hour* by sixty minutes, not *one-hundred*.

Later Mesopotamian traditions viewed Anu in a similar manner as the abstract Babylonian expression of ILU. He became the "Lofty One" or "Supreme God Most High" in the pantheon, a remote, distant and indiscriminate All-Father much more representative of the "Heavenly Father" that Jesus alluded to in the *New Testament* then that of the *Old Testament* God of the Hebrew. Solidity of his personification becomes increasingly faint in descending traditions, and though within his power, he rarely intervenes or makes an appearance to the "earth" world of gods and men. His main function in the pantheon is as the "Father" of the gods, who are then mainly left to deal with material universe on their own accord. From Tablet-A in our "*Anunnaki Bible*":—

When first the gods were [like] men on earth,
Settling on the bond-heaven-earth,
Anu decreed that the Anunnaki would come
  forth...

Few incantation tablets (or "prayers") invoke the powers of *Anu* directly. The heavenly force is perceived as too vast to be channeled directly by successors and to degrade it to anything more accessible would be to compromise the nature of what is represented. In Semitic traditions, the role of Kingship in Heaven is equated to the full extent of power that keeps the universe in motion, contained in an "unspeakable" and "unknowable" name (or "Tetragrammaton" in modern Hebrew-based mysticism—YHVH).

It is more common for the magician or priest to evoke a subsidiary deity from the "pantheon" ("*divine lineage*") to invoke the names known to them rather than pursue methods of Egypto-Hermetic cryptomancy to divine and compel spirits against their will using "true-names." In the Chaldeo-Babylonian tradition, the names of Enki and Marduk are evoked to speak the names—later traditions often used them to replace obscure and "secret" names altogether. As Lenormant explains:

> "True indeed there was a supreme name which possessed the power of commanding the gods and extracting from them a perfect obedience, but that name remained the inviolable secret of *Hea* or EA —Enki. In exceptionally grave cases the magician besought *Hea*, through the mediator *Silik-mulu-khi*—Marduk, to prono-

unce the solemn word in order to re-establish order in the world and restrain [temper] the powers of the abyss. But the enchanter did not know that name, and could not in consequence introduce it into his formulae... he could not obtain or make use of it, he only requested the god who knew it to employ it, without endeavoring to penetrate the terrible secret himself."

Though appearing infrequently in prayers, one example of a magician's "Grand Invocation" addressing Anu appears as a protective incantation at times and then also a hymn of adoration. From *Tablet-P* in *"The Complete Anunnaki Bible"*:—

Anu, King in Heaven, Eternal Prince of the
  Anunnaki,
Whose words are the rule over the *Assembly of
  Anunnaki*,
Lord of the unequaled Horned Crown [*of the
  Starry Heavens*],
You who can travel anywhere in the universe
  on a raging storm;
You who stands in the royal chamber admired
  as a king.
The ears of the IGIGI are directed to hear your
  pure words,
The *Assembly of Anunnaki* gather around thee
  in reverence.

At your command the *Anunnaki* bow to salute;
At your command the wind blows
And food and drink are abundant;
At your command the angry demons
Turn back to their habitations.
May all the gods of Heaven and Earth
Pray at your *Altar of Offering;*
And may the kings of dragonblood on Earth
Give you heavy tribute.
May men pray to you daily and offer sacrifices
    and adoration.
May your heart be at rest and may you ever
    reign righteously.
To the city of *n.* show your abundant favor
    and grace."

The no less significant role of royal "Lady of Heaven" does not appear to be fixed individual. Several female entities are listed at one time or another as consorts of *Anu.* The title-name "*Antu*" is usually given, and much like the name of her husband, her title is more of a role than a proper name (and carries a numerological designation of 55). The "Queen of the Starry Heavens" traditionally rules the cosmos with her partner, but the exact personality associated often it differs by tradition. In one interpretation of the Sumerian *Genesis,* the consort of Anu (or AN) is originally listed as KIA (or KI), the "*Spirit of the Earth*" that "Enlil separated from the heavens."

In a rather romantic Babylonian version, *Anu* bestows the name of I.STAR or *Ishtar* (Sumerian: IN.ANNA)—meaning *"Beloved of Anu"*—onto his grand-daughter, a title-position sharing that of his own consort.

If one were to assume that the ANS*h*AR and KIS*h*AR [parents to AN and KI] represents the pure spirit of *zi-an-na* (spirit of heaven) and *zi-ki-a* (spirit of earth) in the mystical incantations, then we might assume, since not otherwise addressed from the pantheon, that the addendum nearly always added in prayer to the forces (after those just mentioned) are to the manifested "first forms" of both heaven and earth as *zi-dingir-anna* and *zi-dingir-kia*. KANPA is translated from our original *"Mardukite Cypher"* manuscript [as relayed in *"The Complete Anunnaki Bible"*] as either "mark well," "remember" or "conjure" based on references from the last two centuries of revived interest in tablet literature. DINGIR is given as "first-god" or "mighty spirit power."

> *Zi Anna Kanpa*
> *Zi Kia Kanpa*
> *Zi Dingir Anna Kanpa*
> *Zi Dingir Kia Kanpa*

Mystical experiences by modern Mardukites with *Anu* directly have been limited.

Given the archetypal sage-hermit motif attached to him, it can be difficult for the mind to comprehend the force of his "shade." Though it may be the result of poetic licensing, his image of a "King in Heaven" seated on a throne in the clouds can be traced back even to these first spiritual philosophies. Whether or not this is taken literally by an initiate, the fact remains that according to tradition, *Anu* leads the original *Anunnaki* pantheon of Sumerian "elder gods" to earth. For meditations and modern ritual, his sign is often traced as a singular ray (or arrow bolt) descending downward.

— II —

ENLIL : DEMIURGE OF CREATION

After the realms of "heaven" and "earth" had been clearly defined, the great separation or fracture of reality ensued. In fact, the ancient texts quite literally describe this as the "heavens" ("AN"—the eternal all-encompassing space aspect) being "moved away" from "earth" ("KI"—the solidified concentrated matter aspect). This is generally followed by a reiteration—ancient tablet writers seemed to enjoy poetic redundancy—of earth being "separated" from heaven, as evident even in the "*Song of the Hoe*":—

> *Enlil, who will make the human seed of the*
> *Land come forth from the Earth,*
> *And not only did he hasten to separate*
> * Heaven from Earth,*
> *And hasten to separate Earth from Heaven...*

It is customary for Sumerian tablet cycles to begin with the formation of creation and the genealogy of their pantheon even if it did little to contribute to the actual context of the saga.

It is possible that this literary mechanism added credibility epic characters and places set against the background reality of creation, and of course, the "*gods.*" The act may also have been a result of devotion and respect.

In parody we might equate this to—"*First the universe was created, then gods were born and then such and such happened.*" Many of these early tablet cycles include introductory lines that reinforce an understanding of Sumerian cosmogony and spirituality. Judging by the frequency of their appearance, there is little doubt concerning the identity of at least two primary gods of the Sumerian tradition, the first of which we have already mentioned:—

> *After AN had carried off heaven*
> *After EN.LIL had carried off earth*

EN.LIL—["EN"=*Lord*, "LIL"=*Air, Breath, Lofty*] —was the national god of ancient Sumer, essentially displacing (the more distant and less materially concerned) AN (*Anu*) as head of the "Elder Gods" on Earth. *Enlil's* offspring include a majority of the "younger generation" of "*Enlilite*" gods. His "patron-city" or "sacred-city" was Nippur [NI.IBRU], named for the geographic center (or "mid-section") of Mesopotamia, where his temple-ziggurat was built—the E.KUR, "House [like a] Mountain"—the four corners of which represented the quarters of the material world. His consort is also ranked high in the pantheon— NIN.LIL (or in the later form as *Belit*)—a title given to SUD. *Enlil's* designation is 50—"Command of Physical Space"—in Mesopotamian numerology, and the correlating rank for *Ninlil* is 45.

More than simply a "Ruler" of the Organized Universe, *Enlil's* position and title displays him as the original representation of the *"demiurge"* of creation—best known as a "Gnostic" concept, borrowed from Greek and Hermetic Schools—meaning the "designer of the material world" (a title also attributed to *Enki* as *Ptah*, "the Engineer," in Egypt). But, *Enlil* did not personally attend to each and every aspect of this material world. His commanding position enabled him to focus on *management*—overseeing other "spirits," "angels" or Anunnaki that were led down from the "heavens" (or, out of an inter-dimensional existence, *&tc.*) to forge a concrete physical existence on "earth"— like adding paint to a once blank canvas of infinite potentiality. For this, he is the *first* attributed with the power of the number "Fifty," also the number of names (of "angelic" war-generals, bio-engineers, *&tc.*) found on the seventh tablet of the *Enuma Elis*. This is the same "Power of Fifty" attributed as the "names" of *Marduk* in *Babylon*, used to elevate him to the position of "Enlil-ship" [*ell-ilu'tu*] or "Kingship" of the material world.

Enlil's first responsibility in the "new world" was assigning tasks and official designations, some of which seem to have been competed for. Sumerian tablets account for one such instance, introducing us to the forerunners of Cain and Abel, two brothers who rival against one another in an agricultural contest to win the favor of *Enlil* and the position of "farmer-god." Given the peaceful "swords to plow-shares" described in literature from *Enlil's Sumer*, no bloody murder is described at the climax of the story, but instead a simple judgment by *"wise father Enlil,"* which is mutually agreed upon by the the two brothers (Emesh and Enten) and they toast one another with libations! Kramer translates:—

> Enlil answers *Emesh* and *Enten*:
> "The life-producing water of all the lands,
>   *Enten* is its 'knower,'
> As farmer of the gods he has produced
>   everything.
> *Emesh*, my son,
> How dost thou compare thyself with *Enten*, thy
>   brother?"
> The exalted word of Enlil whose meaning is
>   profound,
> The decision taken, is unalterable,
> Who dares transgress it?
> *Emesh* bent the knees before *Enten*,
> Into his house he brought . . . [offerings],
> The wine of the grape and the date.
> *Emesh* presents *Enten* with gold, silver and
>   lapis lazuli.
> In brotherhood and friendship,
> Happily, they pour out libations,
> Together to act wisely and well, they
>   determined.
> In the struggle between *Emesh* and *Enten*,

>   *Enten*, the steadfast farmer of the gods,
>   Having proved greater than *Emesh* . . .
>   . . . O father Enlil, praise!

Another ancient Sumerian epic—the "Creation of the Pickax"—describes *Enlil* giving agricultural tools to "primitive workers" to aid their field-work, keep the populations fed, but also to ensure appropriate offerings of sustenance were being brought to the pyramid-like temple-ziggurats. As a deity in the Anunnaki Pantheon, *Enlil's* role and identity is best reflected in the purely Sumerian texts. He is transferred to the Babylonians as IL.-LIL, to the Assyrians as *Bel* (the original one, anyway) and he even becomes the prototype of the Semitic Yahweh (EL in Hebrew). None of these later forms actually preserve the definitions of his position among the original Sumerians—"Lord God" of the Judeo-Christian *Old* Testament, as Lenormant confirms:—

> "*Hea* [EA–Enki] passed into the Chaldeo-Babylonian [system] without changing his office, character or name, (but) *mul.ge.lal* [Enlil], on the contrary, bore no resem-lance in documents of the magical collect-ion to [his former office] *Bel*, the demiurge and god of the organized universe,with whom he was afterward assimilated, in or-der to find him an equivalent in the religion by which he was adopted."

An apparent dualism later emerged in Mesopotamia, not only between lineages of *Enlil* and *Enki*, but also among political campaigns of the "younger" gods. This "philosophical conflict" is all too easily passed off in people's mind's as "light versus dark" and "good versus evil." But, what we are really given is a "division of reality"—still a singular reality mind you, but divided in consciousness. The *demiurge* of creation is later viewed as the "separator" of the *physical* from the *spiritual* and thus, by mortal standards, the one responsible for manifesting a world of form that is experienced in pain and suffering. While this is not directly reflected in Sumerian spirituality, the evolution of this esoteric tradition later in Mesopotamia (and elsewhere) accompanied a significant analytical (or critical) thought process with subsequent generations. Each had the opportunity to assimilate and revise the system. Sandra Tabitha Cicero summarizes this development—

"*Ellil* was a friend to humanity. However, like the Hebrew god *Yahweh*, his anger could be aroused by human wickedness It was *Ellil* who advocated that gods unleash the Great Flood upon humanity in the story of *Atra-Asis*. The unpleasant task of enforcing human calamities decreed by the gods fell upon *Ellil*. Because of this he has usually been accused of being a severe and destructive deity by later scholars. By contrast, Sumerian hymns venerate him as a gracious father figure who protects his people."

Samuel Kramer translates an example of just such a hymn from the "*Enlil in the E.KUR*" tablets:—

Enlil,
Whose command is far reaching;
Whose "word" is lofty and holy;
Whose pronouncement is unchangeable;
Who decrees destinies unto the distant
  future. . .
The Gods of Earth bow down willingly before
  him;
The Heavenly gods who are on Earth
Humble themselves before him;
They stand faithfully, according to instructions.
Lord who knows the destiny of The Land,
Trustworthy in his calling;
Enlil, who knows the destiny of Sumer,
Trustworthy in his calling;
Father *Enlil,*
Lord of all the lands;
Father *Enlil,*
Lord of the Rightful Command;
Father *Enlil,*
Shepherd of the Black-Headed Ones. . .
From the Mountain of Sunrise
To the Mountain of Sunset,
There is no other Lord in the land;

You alone are King.

We see very little of this venerated mention of *Enlil* specifically within Mardukite literature of the Chaldeo-Babylonian paradigm. When he is respectfully mentioned, it is usually only in the context of the fundamental "Supernal Trinity" [*Anu–Enlil–Enki*] invoked at the head of some incantations.

Most post-Sumerian negative attitudes toward *Enlil* centrally focus on his recorded opposition to the creation of humans, and then their preservation during the *Deluge*.

Modern Mardukite experiences with the *Enlil*-current are subject to self-honesty. Expectations and culturally based biases held firmly in the psyche will have a hold on any literal interpretations. But this is no less present pertaining to mystical work, which requires the magician maintain an degree of absolute purity and self-honesty if "invoking" this energy. This is the very real "god," depicted in the Judeo-Christian *Old Testament*, and is not trivial being. [In other words: weigh your heart against a feather first!] The mystical symbol most with *Enlil* is a downward pointing triangle—a sign of command—possibly a literal representation of energetic flow (downward from above), or else the leadership and power of the Anunnaki "brought down" to Earth.

— III —

ENKI : LORD OF THIS WORLD

The spirito-mystical "Supernal Trinity" composing the most ancient pantheon is concluded with *Enki,* brother of *Enlil.* Anunnaki genealogy records kept by post-Sumerian civilizations emphasize that *Enki* and *Enlil* are actually half-brothers. Both are divine sons of *Anu*—the "Sky-Father"—but as royal heir to "Kingship of Heaven," Enlil is also the son of *Antu*—the "official" consort of *Anu*—while *Enki* is born to *Nammu.* [Other texts reveal *Enlil* as the eldest son of KI and *Enki* as the son of *Antu.*]

Differing Anunnaki lineages play a more significant role among the "younger pantheon" and later dualistic interpretations, but in the original formation of Sumerian civilization, *Enlil* and *Enki* are actually perfect compliments to one another in the division of the material world—Enlil as the ruler of the air and fire aspects, leaving *Enki* the domains of *The Deep*: water and earth.

As the original title suggests, "*Enki*" means, quite literally, "Lord of the Earth"—["EN"=*Lord,* "KI"= *Earth*]—later known as the Babylo-Akkadian epitaph "EA," likely derived from the Sumerian ideograms for "*house*" [E] and "*water*" [A]. This water alignment is suggested further by names for his temple-ziggurat, built in the southern city of

93

Eridu [or *e-ri-dug*—"Home of the Mighty"]
known as both E.ENGURRA ("House of Lower
Waters") or E.ABZU ("House in the Depths").

Where *Enlil* is given a certain authority over the
organization of "space" and management of other
deities, *Enki* is given control over more "worldly
matters" on Earth, and carries the designation of
40. [NINKI or DAMKINA, his consort, is 35.] On
a cosmological level, *Enlil* represents the active
spirit manifest in the world as a whole—or the
why—separated from the "heavens."

By comparison, *Enki* represents more passive elements, but clearly the more condensed "material"
ones solidified on Earth, and also the spirit of *how*
things exist—"hidden" internal engineering, program or "natural design."

> "Here in *Eridu* there was a local deity by
> the name of *Ea*, and the aspiring theolo-
> gians of that city, eager to make him the
> supreme deity of the land, pressed forward
> the claim for lordship over the earth, and in
> an effort to insure his claim applied to him
> the epithet *en-ki*, 'Lord of the Earth,' which
> then became his Sumerian name. But
> though *Enki*, after some centuries, did suc-
> ceed in displacing *Ninhursag* [*Belit, &tc.*]
> and taking third place in the pantheon, he
> failed to topple *Enlil* from his supremacy

and had to settle and had to settle for second best, becoming an *Enlil-banda*, a kind of 'Junior Enlil.' Like other gods he had to travel to *Nippur* to obtain *Enlil*'s blessing after he had built his his temple *E'engurra* in *Eridu*; he had to fill the *Ekur* of *Nippur* with gifts and possessions so that *Enlil* might rejoice with him; though he had charge of the *Me* controlling the cosmos and all civilized life, he had to admit that these were turned over to him by a generous and more powerful *Enlil*."

—S.N. Kramer, *"Sumerian Mythology"*

A 3rd Century B.C. Mardukite Babylonian priest, Berossus, wrote an epic dedicated to the figure *"Oannes,"* a later name for *Enki*. He describes *Enki* establishing the material infrastructure of human civilization, depicted as the "sublime fish god" [*fish = scales = reptilian*] who rises from his ocean home (or in this case, the Erythian Sea near the Persian Gulf) to teach men the crafts necessary for their developmental arts and sciences to flourish. *Enki* is known in *Babylon* as the "Arch-Magus," father of the occult arts and divination, who passed this knowledge to his son, *Marduk*. He served as a patron to those who chose spells and esoteric sciences for combat and is sometimes credited with the original knowledge of magical warfare in the local universe.

In some Chaldeo-Babylonian mystical texts, *Enki* is referred to as "Our Father" in much the same way that the Sumerians referred to *Enlil* and, of course, the much later generation of Mardukites (in the neo-Babylonian period) referred to *Marduk.* Similar properties of *Enki* described in the *Oannes* saga also appear in another tablet cycle, of Babylonian origin—"The World Order of Enki." [Refer to *Tablet-K* in our *"Anunnaki Bible."*] Here, the cuneiform author sets out to list the many innovations of *Enki,* some of which are originally attributed to *Enlil* in earlier Sumerian mythology. "Mardukite" Babylonian Tradition recognized *Marduk* as *Enki's* successor; the finale of another version of the "World Order" tablet concerns "passing over" *Inanna-Ishtar* for a position among *Enki's* roll-call of Babylonian gods. *Enki* answers *Inanna* by documenting implied and bestowed powers she already possesses—but elsewhere from *Babylon,* such as in *Egypt* as the goddess ISIS:—

> *What did I keep from you?*
> *What more could we add to you?*
> *You were put in charge of the crook,*
> *The serpent-staff,*
> *The wand of shepherd-ship.*
> *You interpret the oracular omens of battles*
>   *and combats.*
> *Inanna, you have destroyed what cannot be*
> *destroyed;*

And you have conceived the inconceivable.

A duality between divine brothers—*Enlil* and *Enki* —played a significant role in the establishment of not only human civilization in its physical, fundamental and evolutionary aspects, but also the spiritual and religious philosophies that later emerged on the planet. To point out a widely held, but relatively recent conception (adopted by the Roman Catholic Church): "Yahwist Monotheism." This dictates everything in the universe results from a single being alone, the leader of the "*anakim*" or "*malachim*" [*Anunnaki*] appearing in the Judeo-Christian *Old Testament*. The stature of his being is held above all others who are but intermediaries in the stories.

The position in *heaven*, however, seemed too surreal for accessibility by the priests and prayers of early people, so the pantheists and materialists developed patronage toward the "Lord of the Earth"—representing the powers of the *here and now*, and the necessities and comforts of physical existence: fertility, love, wealth... these all became the domain of *Enki*, whose "secondary" birthright in heaven seems to have transferred to a "primary" one on Earth.

Trailing in the wake of the gods was their sense of "supremacy"—an embedded pyramid-structure turned innate—first used to govern themselves and then left to chosen figureheads and bloodlines on Earth thereafter. This struggle for world domination and power essentially crippled contemporary humans, who simply do not carry enough awakened genetic and intellectual faculties to properly execute such ventures. What efforts have been done in the past, both political and physically combative, have been performed by individuals who actually take these matters very seriously. An investigation into the occult beliefs of the Third Reich will reveal that the Nazis actually adopted very similar beliefs concerning the origins of their race and even connected the Germanic interpretation of the Anunnaki pantheon to the Kings of "*Atlantis*"—meaning they believed in higher minds remaining from a prior civilization.

While it does not condone the actions taken, this fueling belief in "god-blood" and "alien-technologies," however trite it might seem to some readers, allowed Nazi Germany to nearly take over the world. We can see some evidence of this "self-righteousness" throughout history. Many folk have felt as if they were direct physical counterparts acting on behalf of their personal god. The very bloodlines of these gods were believed to flow in the veins of certain kings and temple-priests other lineages, thus representing the power attributed to "heaven," but on "earth." Long before World War II, the Christian Crusades of the Middle Ages were fueled by the same belief—that their god had come in human form and bestowed a decree that "on earth as it is in heaven." Suddenly, "Lord of the Earth" became a highly coveted position, for it was now (from an earthly perspective) just as good as that in "heaven" and more immediately accessible to the people. Titles, icons, powers and attributes of the gods, growing more and more distant in memory with the passage of time, were passed on to specific "royal" and "magical" families—the living embodiments of the "old gods" for Earth's future.

The age of gods passed into that of men. Harmonic dances of grace and beauty once driving a unified Sumer were gone forever, lost to a variegated mix of analytical minds. "Lordship" passed to humans —peace and love all but disappeared from the earth. Rivalry for supremacy in a post-Sumerian world of monotheism resulted in many "tribal" wars in the names of their personal deities. The essence of brotherly love that formed the very systems of physical existence (now being fought over), became separated as "moral dualism"— there was only room for one god now, and the fight for such once political, turned bloody. Of the two brothers, "God" would be associated with all that was orderly, and a "Satan" figure to represent all that was disharmonious. The force of Chaos, first overcome by the Sumerian gods and later tempered to balance creation was now viewed as a source of "evil" and personification of such was passed onto a "devil," originally *brother* of "God." As Semitic peoples near Mesopotamia developed their own traditions, beneficial properties of the Anunnaki, coupled with the personality of *Enlil*, became the figure *Yahweh*. [Yet, the name "EA" clearly has a more similar sound to "*Ia*" or "*Jah*."] The role of *antithesis* was given to *Enki*. Although this association of "evil" and "discordance" is hardly justified, the *Enki* current energetically assimilated this in consciousness—quite simply, he was now the "rebel" among the "elder" pantheon, and it is not surprising that his most famous offspring—*Marduk*—would be a "rebel" son. As a patron, when all of the other gods have said "no," he is the one that might (almost always) say "yes." This is demonstrated not only in the Flood epic (when he went against the will of the *Anunnaki* to secretly preserve his own bloodline), but in any instance when even the gods are petitioning for favors that the others "won't touch."

For magical purposes, many of *Enki's* attributes have since been passed onto the younger generation but in times of extreme need, *Enki* seems to be unparalleled in the ability to "get things done – no matter how." He also seems to allot special time and care for *Inanna-Ishtar* in several tablet-cycles, including her own infamous epic —"*The Descent*." But while rebellious, he was no shady rogue: he was a scientist and philosopher above all else, and the greatest of both among the

Anunnaki (additionally a child of Anu), his skills and bloodline were prized in the "*fashioning*" of the material world—a title he carried in the Egyptian pantheon as PTAH, the "*designer.*"

The mystical symbol used by modern Mardukites to represent the energetic current of *Enki* closely resembles a pyramid or mountain—the KUR. Direction of energy suggested by the symbol is "upward." Movement pools at the surface (or below the surface) and is directed towards the sky. It is an opposite of the sign used for *Enlil.* Both *Enki* and *Marduk* are, at times, depicted as residing within a chamber, pyramid or inhabiting the "*Deep*" [Abyss], all of which are indicative of an "underverse" operating beneath the surface of consciousness or visible material reality. Modern "Mardukite" encounters with the current have been "strong" due to increased modern inclinations of those interested in magic and esoteric sciences. His archetype remains among the most potent alive in systems today. Where the magician is ever seeking the essence of creation or the "words" by which it can be known, in Mardukite tradition, *Enki* is considered that very "*word*" of god made manifest and set free to evolve and unfold in the physical world. Fragments of this spiritual understanding are still maintained in the Semitic Kabbalah—lore which is, even in itself, derived from the original Sumerian Anunnaki "*Tree of Life.*"

— 1 —
NANNA-SIN : "WHO SHINES FOR"

Nanna is listed on Sumerian tablets as eldest of the "younger pantheon," first-born son of *Enlil* and *Ninlil*. His patron city was Ur, where he maintained primary residence at his temple-ziggurat— E.GISH.NU.GAL or *E.Gishshirgal*—"Home of the Throne Seed." He also made frequent appearances in the northern city of *Harran*, where his *E-Khulkhul* temple stood.

Nanna is named for the bright light of the moon gracing the night sky earth, referenced in one epithet as NAM.RA.SIT (*Namrasit*)—"Who Shines Forth." His consort—*Ningal* or *Nikkal*—is the "Great Lady of the Moon," goddess of divination and dreams, the most commonly accessible human "thresholds" to interact with the "*Other.*"

Nanna is credited for prosperity of the ancient Sumerian city of Ur. The early metropolis represented the pure idealism of Sumer as brought to high esteem, long before its legendary destruction from the wrath of *Anu* and *Enlil*. Our ancestors preserved details of these events on cuneiform tablet cycles called "lamentations."

The famous "Lamentation for the Destruction of Ur" tablet is written from the perspective of the "*Lady of Ur,*" or *Ningal*—the consort of *Nanna*.

She relays the sudden sadness that befell the land
the day of the "storm" neared. She sheds tears before AN and *Enlil* that her city "not be destroyed."
But, the assembly of Anunnaki remained *un-
moved*:—

> AN never bent toward those words,
> And Enlil never with, 'It is pleasing, so be it!'
> [To] soothe my heart.

Enlil called down the "storm of heaven" using the
"fire-god"—GIBIL—to assist. The gods "left the
city ruin and the dead were piled up." In despair,
Nanna appeals to his father *Enlil*, asking him to lift
this heavy curse and restore the city to its former
glory. He speaks of the greatness of Sumer and the
love for the people toward their gods. But *Enlil* is
firm, as Thorkild Jacobsen translates:—

> O noble Nanna, be thou (concerned) about
>   yourself,
> What truck [sway] have you with tears?
> There is no revoking a verdict,
> A decree of the assembly,
> A command of AN and Enlil is not known to
> ever change.
> Ur was verily granted kingship
>   but an (ever)lasting [eternal] reign,
> It was not granted.
> You, my Nanna, do not worry. Leave your city!

This description demonstrates the immediate unrest ensuing in Sumer when control is passed to the "younger generation" of *Anunnaki*. The specific reason for the "Destruction of Ur" is conveniently concealed from the tablet saga. Zecharia Sitchin suggests an interesting theory: Since *Nanna* is also known as SU.EN (or "SIN" of later Chaldeo-Babylonian literature), it is possible that he either shares an identity with, or lord over, ZU, a "creature" or "force" that is connected to control of the "Tablets of Destiny" during *Enlil's* possession. That name could be self-proposed to declare *Nanna* as "Lord Zu," or, again, be a reference to control of a serpent-being as EN.ZU—"Lord of the Zu." The name SU.EN might be associated with ZU.EN, or else EN.ZU. The typical persona of *Nanna* as a "gentle father" doesn't appear to match this allocation. It would, however, provide some explanation for why retributive annihilation came down through the leading pantheon, as city-states started to be governed by the "younger generation."

Nanna is given the number 30, correlating to the lunar month—the word "month" is named for the "moon"—and his consort is 25. As eldest of the "zonei" or "younger pantheon" given control of the local solar-system, *Nanna* was given a most prominent celestial domain in conjunction with the earth—the Moon. *Nanna* is actually a shortened version of the more complete designation—*Nannar*, "Light of the Full Moon." As the form of

"SU.EN," he is actually representing the crescent or partial moon, and the Babylonians adopted the name "SIN" from this. The other name "ENZU" is derived from his Akkadian epithet—EN.I.ZUNA —so, the theory mentioned previously is not without some basis.

In Sumerian mythology the moon is held in high regard. Although the primordial chaos cosmologically brings forth the Sun into existence first, as illustrated in nearly all other solar-oriented "Mardukite" systems, the Sumerian Anunnaki chose to represent the Moon with Nanna, a firstborn son of *Enlil* and *Ninlil*, who with his consort *Ningal*, give birth to both *Inanna-Ishtar* (*Venus*) and Shammash (*the Sun*). It is here, as before concerning cosmology represented by pantheistic beings, that we must keep a distinction between the *Anunnaki* "younger pantheon" and the literal "celestial bodies" they are named for. Ancient tablets are quite obscure in this regard, because cuneiform signs for the planets and deities are identical. The people, themselves, were not confused by this, as we might be today when looking back at the tablet records with modern eyes.

In one sense, *Nanna* is described as the "light of the moon." But certainly *Nanna*, the *Anunnaki King of Ur*, was present in his city while simultaneously the light of the moon bore down on the earth at night. The association is clearly a reference to a more ancient cosmogony reflected in Sumerian beliefs: the day was born from the night, and not that the moon literally gave birth to the sun-star of our local system.

As a mystical "energetic current," the *Moon Gate* is traditionally the first that an individual will encounter when crossing the veils of material existence to the veils of negative existence, or the *Abyss*. Ancient Anunnaki denizens of the universe established "veils of existence" when the "material order" was brought or willed into being. They stationed the "younger pantheon" as *Guardians of the Gates*. The moon, as we might expect, is quite vibrant but gently passive and tranquil.

Ningal—the "Lady of the Moon"—receives many of the lunar attributes in later systems—If not by name, then by gender, as most esoteric revivals that do not truly use the combined-counterpart paradigm of a male-god and female-goddess as one essence, usually reduce celestial divinity to polar dualism: a 'masculine' "solar" god and the 'feminine' "lunar" goddess. But, *Sumer*, unlike *Babylon*, was a primarily *lunar*-oriented society and tradition with only subsequent emphasis on the *Sun* and *Venus*. Ancient astronomical symbols found on the oldest Sumerian art renderings for spirituality and astronomy are frequently representations of the *Sun-star*, *Venus* and, in the case of *Nanna-Sin* and *Ningal*—the *lunar crescent*—

which, when depicted above a deity, was often
called the "horns."

* * *

Once an "initiate" passes the "*Earth Gate*" in
search of cosmic truth on the path of "Ascension"
up the *Ladder of Lights*, the lunar current is generally the first one accessed. This is because the
"Moon Gate" is most closely aligned to the familiar astral and dreams "level" of enchantment and
fantasy that many access—even unknowingly. As
an elementary aspect of all mystical work, the
"first degree" is where a seeker is able to actually
realize in consciousness that they are not only their
physical body. Actualization of this basic principle
is not taken for granted, since many do not achieve
even this "degree" of spiritual evolution (or "*unfoldment*") during their lifetime. Yet, in contemporary "new age" traditions, many initiates too often simply stop here, even when they believe they
have moved on from it, remaining enamored with
the infinite potentiality of appearances able to
manifest through dissolution of the first veil. Esoteric instruction given to the Mardukite Chamberlains explains:—

> "The first 'level' encountered (aside from
> the extraordinarily subtle or blatantly phys-
> ical 'Earth Gate') in the system is the Moon
> Gate, which ironically, is the embodiment
> of the 'common' astral plane or dreamscape

that many have already enjoyed lucid access to without formal occult education."

The formal "magical path" has a starting point. A
magician working through the "veils of existence"
connected to and surround us as the systematic
design that keeps the material world "flowing."
But, be warned: opiate-like sensations that the
mind experiences at this level is quite addicting,
and with good reason—it was designed to hold
fast the unbidden minds that drifted into it, whether intentionally or otherwise. It is a veil meant to
be so glamorous that the mere access of it immediately conjures illusions of ascension and enlightenment that are not yet truly manifest. The elation of
initially breaking free of the physical chains can
bring such ecstasy that the naïve neophyte actually
believes they "have arrived," when really they
have just begun. As the enigmatic editor Simon
warns:—

"It is the initiatory plane, and it is here, at
the Lunar Gate, that the vast majority of occultists lose their way, forever. For most
people, it is the repository of every inspirational, delusional, ghostly, spiritual, hallu-
cinogenic event that has ever transpired in
their lives. The temptation of this plane is
to become one of those vague, ethereal
types one finds spouting psychobabble on
morning talk shows. Many channelers are

victims of staying too long on the Lunar level; astral puppets who never progress beyond sitting on the ventriloquist's lap. . . instead of mastering this plane, it has become *their* master; every breeze that brushes across their faces become a caress from beyond, every news item a direct message from an entity on Alpha Centauri. Avoid them like the very plague . . ."

Astral "shade-forms" of *Nanna-Sin* and *Ningal* reflect an archetypal otherworldly "fairy" king and queen—born of heaven, ruling on earth and embodied in the lunar threshold connecting between the two. Most mystics encountering these personas have seen them in their elderly form, but the blue-hued moonlight radiating from their skin gives off so much beauty that we tend to think of them as ageless. The color associated with the moon is silver and the essence and symbol attributed to *Nanna* is the royal wand or scepter of lapis lazuli.

When the moon was not visible, it was thought to be dwelling in the underworld. When a lunar eclipse occurred, Sumerian tradition described the moon battling wicked demons before reappearing. This more active face of the lunar current is not often tapped by most "magical" tables of correspondence. We can find similar beliefs concerning disappearance-and-appearance of *Sun* and *Moon* throughout many ancient cultural mythologies.

The Mardukite "Invocation of the Nanna Gate" (given in the "*The Complete Anunnaki Bible*") very closely resembles an incantation found from the tablet-series known to scholars as: "Prayers of the Lifting of the Hand."—the entire basis for L.W. King's "*Babylonian Magic & Sorcery.*" The original prayer is as follows:—

O SIN! O *Nannar*! Mighty One . . . [among the gods]
siptu ilu-SIN ilu-NANNARU ru-su-bu u- . . .

O SIN, who art unique, thou that brightens . . . [the heavens]
ilu-SIN id-dis-su-u, mu-nam-mir . . .

That gives light unto the nations . . . [over the four lands]
sa-ki-in na-mir-ti a-na nisi- . . .

That unto the black-headed race art favorable . . . [god to your people]
ana nisi sal-mat kakkadu us-su-ru sa- . . .

Bright is thy light, in heaven . . . [like fire]
nam-rat urru-ka ina sami-i . . .

Brilliant is thy torch, like the fire-god . . . [burning brightly]
sar-hat di-pa-ra-ka, kima ilu-GIBIL . . .

Thy brightness fills the broad earth!
ma-lu-u nam-ri-ru-ka irsita(ta) rapasta

The brightness of the nations he gathers, in
thy sight . . .
  sar-ha nisi uk-ta-sa-ra ana a-ma-ri-ka

O *Anu* of the sky, whose purpose no man
learns!
  *ilu-A-nim sami-i sa la i-lam-ma-du mi-lik-
  su ma-*

Overwhelming is thy light like the Sun-god
[*Shammash*], thy first born!
  su-tu-rat urru-ka kima ilu-Samas bu-uk-ri-

Before thy face the great gods bow down, the
fate of the world is set before thee!
  *kan-su pani-ka ilani rabuti purus matati
  sakin(in) ina pani-ka*

In the evil of an eclipse of the Moon which in
X month on *X* day, has taken place,
  *ina lumin ilu-atali ilu-SIN sa ina arhi pulani
  umi pulani isakna(na)*

In the evil of the powers, of the portents not
good, which are in my palace and my land,
  *lumun idati iti.mis limniti la tabati sa ina
  ikalli-ya u mati-ya ibasa-a*

The great gods beseech thee and thou gives
counsel!
  ilani rabuti i-sal-lu-ka-ma tanadin(in) mil-ka

They take their stand, all of them, they petition
at thy feet!

izzizu pu-hur-su-nu us-ta-mu-u ina sapli-ka

O SIN, glorious one of IKUR! They beseech
thee and thou givest the oracle of the gods!
*ilu-SIN su-pu-u sa I.KUR i-sal-lu-ka-ma ta-
mit ilani tanadin(in)*

The end of the month is the day of thy oracle,
the decision of the great gods;
*bubbulum u-um ta-mit-ti-ka pi-ris-ti ilani
rabuti*

The thirtieth day is thy festival, a day of prayer
to thy divinity!
*umu XXX-kan i-sin-na-ka u-um ta-sil-ti ilu-
ti-[ka]*

O God of the New Moon, in might unrivaled
whose purpose no man learns,
*ilu-Namrasit i-muk la sa-na-an sa la i-lam-
ma-du mi-lik-su ma- . . .*

I have poured thee a libation of the night
(with) wailing, I have offered thee (with)
shouts of joy a drink offering of . . . [*type
of drink*]
*as-ruk-ka si-rik musi lallartu ak-ki-ka ri-is-
ta-a si-kar . . .*

I am bowed down! I have taken my stand! I
have sought for thee!
kan-sa-ku az-za-az a-si-ka ka- . . .

Do thou set favor and righteousness upon me!
ka-sa dum-ki u mi-sa-ri sukun(un) ili-[ya]

May my god and my goddess, who for long
have been angry with me,
*ili-ya u ilu-istari sa is-tu u-um ma-du-ti is-
bu-su*

In righteousness and justice deal graciously
with me! Let my way be favorable, with
joy . . .
*ina kit-ti u misari lis-li-mu itti-ya ur-hi lid-
mi-ik had-is ni- . . .*

And ZA.GAR, the god of dreams hath sent,
u-ma-'-ir-ma ilu-ZA.GAR ilu sa sunati

In the night season . . . [cleanse me of] my sin,
my iniquity may . . . [it be absolved]
*ina sat musi Kab.mis ar-ni-ya lu-us-mi sir-ti
lu-ta*

For ever may I bow myself in humility before
thee!
ana da-ra-ti lud-lul da-li-li-[ka]

— 2 —

NABU : "WHO SPEAKS FOR"

Mythologists and mythographers often associate the Sumerian "Lord of the Tree of Life" [*Ningishzidda*] with the Egyptian deity "Thoth"— the archetypal Mercurial current shared by Hermes, Merlyn, Ogmios, *&tc.*, but the most iconic *Anunnaki* "messenger of the gods" more appropriately corresponds to a more "Mardukite" character in Babylon. If one carefully considers the "divine" occupation of this lineage in Egypt, there is evidence for a "third party" of gods, apart from strict *Enlil* and *Enki* lineages, that most strongly influenced the Babylonian system in preference over the former Sumerian one.

In the Babylonian tradition, the "Apollonian herald of the mercurial current" among the "younger pantheon" is the *heir-son* of *Marduk* and *Sarpanit* —*the* patrons of *Babylon*. This role is attributed to *Nabu*—also rendered *Nebo* or *Nabak* in Semitic language—meaning "spokes-person." He shares residence at the temple-ziggurat of the city of *Borsippa* [*Birs-i-Nimrud*] (approximately ten miles from *Babylon*) with his consort, *Tasmit—Teshmet-(um)* or *Tashmitu*. In addition to managing the national school and temple of scribe-priests, *Nabu* and *Teshmetu* made annual visits to *Babylon* for the celebration of the "New Year" [A.KI.TI or "Akitu"] festival held on the spring equinox.

Nabu is the original "scribe of the gods," a patron deity of wisdom-knowledge and writing, inventor of the "reed-stylus" (*pen*), and the first truly refined form of cuneiform—distinguishing the stylus-script of *Babylon* from early pictograms of *Sumer*. His energetic current carries an affinity to Mercury—communication, divination and the air element. Semitic-Hebrew language incorporated the word "*Nabih*," meaning "prophet." *Nabu* is effectively the "*Prophet of Marduk*" and a "*Messianic Son*" for Mardukites of *Babylon*. Priests and kings evoked his name in the consecration of their libraries, asking him to bless their hands when writing tablets and also to curse those who might steal or desecrate the libraries. The intellectual nature of *Nabu* and his unusual type of psychological warfare are echoed on an ancient basalt tablet, the "*Caillou Michaux*," named for the archaeologist excavating it for the French National Museum:—

> *May Nebo, the supreme intelligence,*
> *overwhelm him with affliction and terror,*
> *and lastly may he hurry him into incurable*
> *despair.*

When the ancient Mardukites were losing ground to Enlilite-Yahwists during the "Old Testament" biblical era, *Nabu* was charged with the task of maintaining a tradition of *Marduk's* followers near *Babylon* and in *Egypt*. Several neo-Babylonian Kings of the time period are also given related names in patronage and reverence to the younger pantheon of the Mardukites, such as: Nabuna'id (*"Nabu is exalted"*), Nabupolassar (*"Nabu protects his son"*) and, of course, Nebochadnezzar (*"Nabu preserve my first-born son"*), just to name a few. For the Mardukites in Babylon, *Nabu* represented a "messianic prophet"—born of a "Heavenly King" (*Marduk*) and *Enki's* special hybrid off-spring (*Sarpanit*), long before Semitic and Christian lore existed to record such things, but un-doubtedly serving as an inspirational source to later traditions.

Although an old soul—a steward of all wisdom of the gods, responsible for recording their "move-ments" in a Mesopotamian version of the "Book of Life" and the famous "Tablets of Destiny"—*Nabu* is actually a relatively young "deity"of the Mar-dukite Anunnaki pantheon. His other epithet —"TU.TU"—appears notably as the thirteenth name (of the Fifty) from the *"Enuma Elis"* (found on Mardukite *Tablet-F* in the *"Anunnaki Bible"*); the thirteenth name that Marduk assumed unto himself during the *"Epic of Creation."* The "name" of this "power" is transferred to *Nabu* in the Baby-lonian Mardukite Tradition, although the govern-ing domain is quite ambiguous:

Nabu-Tutu,
He who created them anew,
And should their wants be pure,
Then they are satisfied.

This intellectual riddle described the very function *Nabu* serves—the recording of life, history, people... and *gods*—the "eye-of-the-beholder" concerning descendants of the Anunnaki, origins of humanity and courses of life and existence— were now *Nabu's* to hold. He could create them anew, give anyone a new face and past and there- fore future. He was the "*Voice of God*"—the mes- senger frequency-wave of the highest brought to the lowest and an intermediary between.

Mesopotamian religion held a firm inseparable view of male-female aspects in divinity, but the re- lationship between *Nabu* and *Tasmit* (or *Teshmet*) is truly complimentary—where *Nabu* is a projector of communication, *Tasmit* is a receiver. She is the Babylonian "goddess of hearing," the one who listens to the prayers—often sought as a "*transmit- or*" to her husband and the other deities. A powerful incantation to "*Tesmitu*" is found on the reverse-side of the prayer-tablet referenced previ- ously for *Nanna*. The incantation is specifically a petition to "remove sickness and enchantments caused by an eclipse of the Moon":—

O Lady Tasmitu!
I ___ , son of ___ and ___,

Whose god is ___ , whose goddess is ___ ,
In the evil of an eclipse of the Moon,
Which in ___ month on ___ day has taken
  place,
In the evil of the powers, of the portents,
Evil and not good, which are in my palace and
  my land,
I have turned towards thee! I have established
  thee!
Listen to the incantation!
Before *Nabu*, thy spouse, the lord, the prince,
The firstborn son of the E.SAGILA, intercede
  for me!
May he hearken to my cry at the word of thy
  mouth;
May he remove my sighing;
May he learn of my supplication!
At his mighty word,
May god and goddess deal graciously with me!
May the sickness of my body be torn away;
May the groaning of my flesh be consumed!
May the consumption of my muscles be re
  moved!
May the poisons that are upon me be loosened!
May the ban be torn away and the curse
  consumed!
May the Anunnaki come forth and demand
  justice!
At thy command, may mercy be established!
May god and king ordain favor

At thy mighty command that is not altered,
And thy true mercy that changes not,
  O Lady Tasmitu!

* * *

Perhaps one of the most fundamental lessons to be learned via the mercurial current is *discernment*. Once the veils have been penetrated and the spectral showers of vast images and illusions are tapped on the lunar level, *temperance* is required. Where the *Moon Gate* provides access to the "magical path," the *Mercury Gate* (*"Nabu Gate"*) is the beginning of the "mystical path," concerning the "Secret Doctrines of the Cosmos" contained on the "Tablets of Destiny." *This* wisdom dissolves half-truths of worldly programming, encoding and other glamours. True knowledge replaces all erroneous (mis)information. [This is the subject of Mardukite Systemology *Liber-One*, titled *"Tablets of Destiny"* by Joshua Free.]

Our intellect causes psychosomatic effects on our emotional state, which in turn influences our behavior. The methodology suggested taps undefiled unconditioned stimuli from beyond the veil of tangible experiential based memory data. This ensures a higher rate of success generating transcendental moments of *"true gnosis,"* and not merely trivial enlightenment-delusions of false-light. The *light on the screen* can be made to be seen for what it is. The "weight of wisdom" often causes *Nabu* to appear relatively much older than he actually is. His number is twelve, a fundamental value to the "*sexagesimal*" (Base-60) mathematics of Mesopotamia, a method still used today to denote time, angles, locales and speed of travel across any space. His traditional color is blue, and in addition to the "reed stylus," *Nabu* is represented by the double-barred cross, also visible in his cuneiform sign: PA (as seen on the logo for *JFI Publishing*).

The traditional Mardukite invocation made to *Nabu* (as seen in "*The Complete Anunnaki Bible*") resonates strongly with the twenty-second prayer from the "*Lifting of the Hand*" cuneiform tablet series:—

O hero, prince, first-born of *Marduk*!
  siptu rubu asaridu bu-kur ilu-Marduk

O prudent ruler, offspring of *Zarpanitu*!
  Massu-u i-ti-ip-su i-lit-ti ilu-ZARPANITU

O *Nabu*, bearer of the Tablet of Destiny of the gods, Director of the E.SAGILA!
  Ilu-Nabu na-as duppu si-mat ilani a-sir E.SAG.ILA

Lord of E.ZIDA, Shadow of Borsippa,
  bil E.ZID.DA su-lul duru-BORSIPPA-ki

Darling of IA [Enki], Giver of Life,

na-ram ilu-IA ka-i-su balatu

Prince of Babylon, Protector of the Living,
asarid BAB.ILI na-si-ru na-pis-ti

Lofty Lord of the hill-dwelling, fortress of the
nations, Lord of temples!
ilu du-ul da-ad-mi kar misi bil is-ri-ti

Thy name is the word in the mouth of the
people, O sedu ["friendly spirit"]
zi-kir-ka ina pi nisi su.dub.ba ilu-sidu

O son of the mighty prince *Marduk*, in thy
mouth is justice!
mar rubi rabi ilu-Marduk ina pi-ka kit-ti

In thy illustrious name, at the command of thy
mighty godhead,
*ina si-ik-ri-ka kabti ina ki-bit ilu-ti-ka
rabiti(ti)*

I ___ , the son of ___ and ___ , who am
smitten with disease, thy servant,
*ana-ku pulanu apil pulani mar-su sum-ru-su
arad-ka*

Whom the hand of the demon and breath of the
wicked [spirit has seized],
*sa kat utukki-ma imat bur.ru.da nam-kil-lu-
ni-ma nal-susu-ni*

May I live, may I be perfect [with your
wisdom]
lu-ub-lut lu-us-lim-ma . . . gub.bu.du

luksud(ud)

Set justice in my mouth!
su-us-kin kit-ti ina pi-ya

[Kindle] mercy in my heart!
sup-si-ka damikti(ti) ina libbi-ya

May the Anunnaki return and be established!
  May they command mercy!
ti-i-ru u an.nu.na.ki man-za-[za lik-bu-u]
  damikti(ti)

May my god stand at my right hand!
li-iz-ziz [ili-ya] ina imni-ya

May my goddess stand at my left hand!
li-iz-ziz [ilu-istari-ya] ina sumili-ya

May the favorable sidu [spirit], the favorable
lamassu [guardian spirit] be with me!
ilu-sidu damiktu ilu-lamassu damiktu . . . -kis
  illi-ya

— 3 —

INANNA-ISHTAR : "QUEEN IN
THE HEAVENS"

Known in *Egypt* as "Goddess of Ten-Thousand Names," a unique position of "*Queenship of Heaven*" is reserved by one of the "younger pantheon" in both Sumerian and later Chaldeo-Babylonian systems. Daughter of *Nanna* and *Ningal*—the Sumerian aspects of the Moon—and twin to *Shammash* (the Sun), this title of high esteem is passed on to a young "Lady of the Stars"—unequaled in beauty and cunning use of divine politics. In ancient Sumer, she is introduced in the original cuneiform literature as IN.ANNA—"*Lady of Anu*" and "*Queen of Heaven.*"

Inanna quickly rises in status as the "archetypal goddess" on earth. She simultaneously represents both a "goddess of love" and "goddess of war," granting her significant domain in the physical world. As a result, she was favored among the masses adoring her for her influence. She is originally given a numeric designation of 5 in Sumer —but in Mardukite Babylon she receives 15, replacing the position held by *Ninmah* (*Ninhursag*) from the elder pantheon. She remains a primary goddess in Assyro-Babylonian tradition, with the name I.STAR (or *Ishtar*)—"The Goddess"—*istari* being the Akkadian word for "goddess." Her traditional/ceremonial color is sometimes white (*Inanna*) and sometimes light-green (*Venus*).

Assyrian art frequently depicts *Inanna-Ishtar* with wings. The same winged form is visible on her Egyptian form as *Isis*. Clearly she was a goddess of the aerial world, not only the *"Anunit-(um)"* (*"Anu's Beloved"*), but literally a "queen" of the skies, stars or heavens. Mythological cycles describe seven objects connected to Ishtar for her aerial travels. Similarly, there are seven garments and ornaments removed during her "Descent to the Underworld." It is quite likely that these items are related to her position as "Lady of the Stars" or "Queen of Heaven"—power symbols associated with this role. Mystical revivalists consider this symbolism significant for modern ritual magic activities reviving Mesopotamian-based ceremonialism (and the Underworld), but perhaps they have an even greater unseen esoteric relevance. In the cuneiform tablet cycle of *Ishtar's* "Crossings to the Underworld"—give as Mardukite *Tablet-C* in our *"Anunnaki Bible"*—these objects are referred to as seven "Divine Decrees" that she "fixes" to her body. They are listed as:—

1. Shugurra – Starry Crown of Anu (on her head)
2. Wand of Lapis Lazuli (in her hand)
3. Necklace of Lapis Lazuli (around her neck)
4. Bag of Brilliant-Shinning-Stones (carried)

5. Gold Ring of Power (on her finger)
6. Frontlet Amulet (as a breastplate)
7. The Pala – Royal Garments (worn about her body)

Zecharia Sitchin interprets the talismans somewhat differently, describing "Seven Objects" of *Inanna* as implements "necessary for traveling the skies":

1. *Shu.gu.ra* – she put on her head
2. Measuring pendents – on her ears
3. Chains of small blue stones – around her neck
4. Twin stones – on her shoulders
5. A golden cylinder – in her hands
6. Straps – clasping her breast
7. *Pa.la* garment – clothed around her body

Genealogies of Sumer detail *Inanna* as a "fourth generation" Anunnaki figure—daughter of *Nanna*, born of *Enlil*, son of *Anu*—and is therefore the "great-granddaughter" of *Anu*. She receives a special place in his heart, which proves beneficial in her rise to power. Even more than this, *Inanna* is a tenacious, actively determined personality that stops at nothing to acquire what she deems rightfully hers. If she wants it, she will take it. In the mythic cycles, this includes "decrees of heaven," "decrees of earth," "secret names of gods" and everything in between. In many ways, her post-Sumerian cult following rivaled *Marduk* for supremacy in *Babylon*. She quite effectively used these powers to win an eternal loyalty from mortals in exchange for granting select worldly desires. The kings she favored, she would stand beside in battle and those she did not (or who fell out of favor) she would lend aid to the opposing side, proving that this "goddess of love" is not to be scorned.

The actual truth of how this "archetypal goddess" figure rose to high power is not so widely known. Her many names have, however, become legendary—not only in Mesopotamia as *Inanna* and *Ishtar*, but elsewhere as *Isis*, *Aphrodite*, *Venus*, *Astarte*, *Metis*, *Brigit* (among countless other names) —marking her widespread appearance among many diverse cultures. Later religious misogynists could not recognize such vast power as a female form, transferring her identity to *Ashtoreth* or *Astoroth*—a leader of an allegedly "demonic" hierarchy of angels in the Judeo-Christian Semitic and Kabbalistic systems.

The original Sumerian tablet cycle involving *Inanna* and *Enki* is academically called *"The Transfer of the Arts of Civilization from Eridu to Erech."* Seeking greater abundance and power for her city, Inanna travels to *Eridu*—the residence of *Enki*—in pursuit of secret knowledge, holy relics and tablets of power that will enable her to achieve this. Her charm, coupled with the looseness that comes with heavy drinking, won over *Enki*, who gave up some one-hundred decrees and treasures in his compromised state. These are then loaded onto her "Boat of Heaven" and transported back to *Erech*, intermittently making seven rest stops along the way. Realizing what he's done soon after, *Enki* immediately sends his counselor *Isimud* with a host of monsters in pursuit of *Ishtar*, but the damage is done and she arrives safely in *Erech* with her new found "decrees" intact.

We might compare this account to the acquisition of power by *Isis* in Egypt, as deTraci Regula describes:—

> "Her skill as a magician was employed when she sought to receive the sacred true name of Ra, her father in some stories. Ra was ignoring the needs of humanity and Isis resorted to a drastic act of magic, creating a small snake from the exudation of his body, which bit him. To stop the pain, Ra agreed to give Isis his most secret name, allowing her to restore balance."

A romantic patina for *Inanna-Ishtar* is toned by the Romeo-and-Juliet-motif in the relationship with her *consort—Damuzi* (*Dumuzi*) [Sumerian; "*the good son*"] or in Babylon, TAMMUZ "*the good shepherd.*" There are different accounts of their courtship activities and later involvement with the Underworld. [See also Mardukite *Tablet-U* in "*The Complete Anunnaki Bible.*"] One version describes how *Inanna-Ishtar* was head-over-heels overtaken with *Damuzi* from the start. However, another tablet series explains that at the beginning, the "shepherd-god"—*Damuzi*—is rivaling with a "farmer-god" for her love and affections. Not surprisingly, *Damuzi* is actually the youngest son of *Enki*, and apart from *Marduk*, *Nabu* and few others, he was an "officially" acceptable spouse in the tradition of Anunnaki "succession." This was later maintained among the "younger generation" via a combination of the two lineages—in this case a daughter of *Enlil* and a son of *Enki*.

Inanna-Ishtar's rise to power was by no means an arbitrary event. Its significance affected the history of the Anunnaki, but also the evolution of civilization as a whole—the politics, religious beliefs and spiritual traditions. She even maintained high recognition as a patron of Babylon. But it was not the *position* itself that changed the fate of the planet—it was, instead, the *responsibilities* that came along with it.

Anunnaki tradition held the "succession" matter as of highest importance for maintaining domain leadership. It became customary for the "younger generation" lineages of Enlil and Enki to commingle. For Ishtar, it was *Marduk*—heir of *Enki*—that was her intended spouse. Each perfectly complimented one another as the *apex leadership* of the younger pantheon. But, neither party seemed interested in maintaining this obligation as a "team"—so, it never occurred. The role of consort was passed onto *Enki's* youngest son, *Dumuzi*. It initially seemed that everyone agreed to this arrangement, but it resulted in fracturing the powers, creating a third party of gods. The Anunnaki lineage of *Enki* separated—splitting in twain—the followers of *Marduk* versus worshipers of *Ishtar* throughout the ancient world.

When Marduk retreats to *Egypt* to regain supremacy of his own "Mardukite" tradition, Ishtar sets her sights on making the powers *there* her own as well. We can certainly see evidence for a significant influence that ISIS provides for our contemporary general understanding of *Egypt*. The "fighting" that erupts between "brothers" thereafter may be of a similar theme to what is alluded in the "farmer-god versus shepherd-god" stories (concerning Ishtar's courtship of a mate). *Ishtar's* "undying love" for *Dumuzi* is explicitly expressed. Quarreling among the family reaches climactic heights when *Dumuzi* drowns under uncertain circumstances. It is then that Ishtar marches on *Marduk* (known as "*Ra*" there, to the Egyptians), arriving with the Horus-Seth tribes—fracturing the pantheon in Egypt too; Zecharia Sitchin explains:

"The first presence of *Inanna/Ishtar* in Egypt is mentioned in the Edfu text dealing with the First Pyramid War. Called there *Ashtoreth* (her Canaanite name), she is said to have appeared on the battlefield among the advancing forces of Horus. . . as long as the fighting was only between descendants of *Enki*, no one saw a particular problem in having a granddaughter of *Enlil* around. But after the victory of Horus, when Seth occupied lands not his, the situation changed completely: the Second Pyramid War pitched the sons and grandchildren of *Enlil* against the descendants of *Enki*."

* * *

Mystical experiences with *Inanna-Ishtar's* "Venusian" energy current are prevalent throughout the ages across nearly all ancient cultures. She is favored by priests and priestesses of many esoteric and occult traditions many times over for thousands of years. As a self-made "goddess queen" of the *Heavens* and the material domains—love, lust, war, magic—her coveted position of influence is unparalleled among the pantheon. It becomes clear why her intended betrothed was *Marduk*, but as they rivaled for control of the same side of the same coin, they became, in actuality, the same side of two coins.

Although Mesopotamian literature provides a wide array of Anunnaki activity, the colorful picture portrayed in the original system is *"amoral"* or concerns a "*higher ethic*" than readily discernible in mortal life. In fact, this "*utilitarian*" ideal, for better or worse, is demonstrated by most any "higher order" of "authority," which is often mysterious to those it governed. In some form—physically and in memory—the "younger pantheon" of Anunnaki were the "gods" of earth religions for thousands of years, even preferred (in contrast to their elders) for their worldly material accessibility.

As Guardian of the *Venus Gate*, *Inanna-Ishtar* is encountered on the mystic path as a "moral" challenge to rise above the pleasures of earth and seek a higher spiritual *Pathway to Self-Honesty* and *Self-Actualization* beyond the *Human Condition*. Should the initiate succumb to the worldly trappings and temptations, she will undoubtedly enable such with worldly "rewards"—but there is a strict clause to receiving such personal attention and this is well known to master occultists:—

Inanna-Ishtar takes her own for her own,
And that once chosen by her,
No man may take another bride.

There is no shortage of Babylonian tablets revealing prayers, rites and incantations in honor of *Ishtar*. Her allied tradition in *Babylon* consists of the same offerings that priests and priestesses offered *Marduk*—the sprinkling of pure waters, libations and potent beverages, fragrant oils, honey and butter with bread, with sacred woods burning as incense. The number "*seven*" frequently appears in these ancient ceremonies—it was often customary to present a food or drink offering seven times. In other instances, such as "*pure waters,*" offerings are sprinkled about the ground. Other times, vials and jars were left at an "*Altar of Offerings*" dedicated to a specific deity. Once the gods physically left, people on earth retained only memories of their existence, but temple-priests (and their families) were continuously sustained thereafter, living on the offerings that once supported the physical existence of great Anunnaki figures.

Like other examples, invocation-prayers to Ishtar used by modern Mardukites, (including those found in the companion to Liber-50, "*The Complete Book of Marduk by Nabu*") are similar to those found on the "*Prayers of the Lifting of the Hand*" tablet-series from the Kuyunjik collection:

O *Ishtar*, good is thy supplication, when the spirit of thy name is propitious [favorable].
[ilu-ISTAR] ta-a-bu su-up-pu-u-ki ki-i ki-ru-ub nis sumi-ki

Thy regard is prosperity, thy command is light!
[nap]-lu-us-ki tas-mu-u ki-bit-ki nu-u-ra

Have mercy on me, O *Ishtar*! Command abundance!

rimi-nin-ni-ma ilu-ISTAR ki-bi-i na-ha-si

Truly pity me and take away my sighing.
ki-nis nap-li-si-in-ni-ma li-ki-i un-ni-ni-ya

Thy [feet or hands(?)] have I held: let me bring
joy of heart!
sar-ta-a-ki a-hu-zu lu-bi-il tu-ub libbi- . . .

I have borne thy yoke: do thou give [me]
consolation!
u-bil ap-sa-na-ki pa-sa-ha suk- . . .

I have [held] thy head: let me enjoy success
and favor!
u-ki-' kakkadu-ki li-si-ra sa-li-mu

I have protected thy splendor: let there be good
fortune and prosperity!
as-sur sa-ru-ra-ki lu-u tas-mu-u u ma-ga-ru

I have sought thy light: let my brightness
shine!
is-ti-'-u nam-[ri]-ir-ri-ki lim-mi-ru zi-mu-u-a

I have turned towards thy power: let there be
life and peace!
as-hur bi-lut-ki [lu]-u balatu u sul-mu

Propitious be the favorable spirit who is before
thee: may the *lamassu* that goes behind thee
be propitious!
*lu tas-lim ilu-sidu damiktu sa pa-ni-ki sa ar-
ki-ki a-li-kat ilu-lammassu lu tas-lim*

That which is on thy right hand, increase good
  fortune: that which on thy left hand, attain
  favor!
  *sa im-nu-uk-ki mis-ra-a lu-us-sip dum-ka
  lu-uk-su-da sa su-mi-lu-[uk-ki]*

Speak and let the word be heard!
  ki-bi-ma lis-si-mi zik-ri

Let the word I speak, when [spoken], be
  propitious!
  *a-mat a-kab-bu-u ki-ma a-kab-bu-u lu-u ma-
  ag-rat*

Let health of body and joy of heart be my daily
  portion!
  *ina tu-ub siri u hu-ud lib-bi i-tar-ri-in-ni u-
  mi-sam*

My days prolong, life bestow: let me live, let
  me be perfect, let me behold thy divinity!
  *umi-ya ur-ri-ki ba-la-ta surki lu-ub-lut lu-us-
  lim-ma lu-us-tam-mar ilu-[ut-ki]*

When I plan, let me attain (my purpose):
  Heaven be thy joy, may the Abyss hail thee!
  *i-ma u-sa-am-ma-ru lu-uk-su-ud samu-u
  hidutu-ki apsu li-ris-[ki]*

May the gods of the world be favorable to
  thee: may the great gods delight thy heart!
  *ilani sa kis-sa-ti lik-ru-bu-ki ilani rabuti lib-
  ba-ki li-tib-[bu]*

— 4 —

SHAMMASH : "THE SHINNING ONE"

Ancient Mesopotamian astronomers correctly depicted the *Sun* in the middle-center of the "*Ladder of Lights*"—a stream of energies connecting our physical world to the ALL via a "*bridge*," often represented by "Celestial Bodies." Assuming the esoteric chronology that begins with the "*Earth Gate*," the Seeker approaches Gates of local planetary systems—those relatively closer to the Earth: the *Moon*, *Mercury* and *Venus*—and then the *Sun*. According to Sumerian cosmology (and lineage tablets), the *Sun*—or more accurately, the "*sun-god*"—was a twin brother to Inanna-Ishtar (*Venus*), the "Morning Star" born of *Nanna* (*the Moon*). This general course also follows with a worldview that "day was born from night" and more esoterically that "light emerges to penetrate the darkness."

The role of the "*sun-god*" as the physical and spiritual "illuminator" carried the very name given to the "face of the sun"—the Anunnaki sky-commander "UTU" or "UDDU" (Sumerian for "*shinning one*"). The same appears on cuneiform tablets in Akkadian and Chaldeo-Babylonian languages as "*Samas*"—often written as it is pronounced: "S*hammash*"—and "*Babbar*" in some sources. His consort is AYA or AIA (also "*Shendira*")—from the Akkadian for "*dawn.*" Together they shared a sanctuary at *Larsa* (in Sumer); and also a temple in *Sippar* (near Babylon), where the couple eventually retired. *Shammash* is given the Anunnaki designation of "20" and reign of the solar domain —the task of maintaining order as chief of the Anunnaki "Judges"—governing justice, law, balance and truth. [In fact, the "*Shammash*" title was used by Medieval Jewish communities to designate a person that assisted in maintaining a governing order. The name was even used later to designate a "temple servant."]

Shammash—and the *Sun*—are called forth frequently with incantations from mystical and religious cuneiform tablets from the *Ancient Near East*. However, as in many ways a subordinate to other entities in the Anunnaki pantheon, the system as a whole can hardly be considered "sun-worship" in the conventional sense or in the most convenient terms. "Astral" perhaps. It might even more accurately be described as ancient "stellar-worship"—if we are to even ascribe the misunderstood word "worship" to this system at all. All primary "*Olympian*"-type deities of this tradition were either named for celestial objects, or we must assume they named the planets after themselves. We can be sure, however, that the *Sun* played a significant role in the "order" of the material world —a "conqueror of evil" (considered sleeping or battling demons at night) or the "protector of travelers" by day, ceaselessly keeping watch over man's daily activities and work-life. The *Sun* clearly became a popular force for the masses to call upon, as Lenormant describes:—

> "The sun was not one of the highest gods of the religious system which had served as a foundation for *Accadian* magic, his power did not approach that of the three great spirits of the zones of the universe [governed by the Supernal Trinity]. But it was just his lower rank that made him more accessible to the prayers of man; and the fact that his influence upon man and the phenomena of life was so sensibly felt, made them assign to him the office of ar-biter of events and of fate; while lastly, as he dissipated darkness, and consequently was engaged in a struggle with the bad spirits, he became one of the supernatural personages to whom the magical invoca-tions were most frequently addressed."

*　*　*

The "*Sun Gate*" is a significant threshold "cross-ing" on the mystic path. Many do not reach this far in their spiritual evolution (or "ascension proc-ess"). Many are too enamored by trappings of lower realms to reach (and survive) the self-anni-hilation prominent at this Gate. This veil is bright and shinning—it will surely illuminate any "darkness" within you that is still waiting to be purged, in addition to any other physical and sensation-based delights remaining from the Venusian initiation.

In the Egyptian mythic cycle associated with the *Sun*—Yes, there is "Ra," actually a representative of a "*sun behind the sun*" (even more than our local sun), but more important to our topic is the "Osirian mythos" of death and transformation—the "solar-judge" weighing the soul to measure impurity. The initiate must allow the pictures and images of their "former" programmed existence to be burned away—allow the baggage and energetic attachments of a "lower life" to be dissolved.

> "*I come in self-annihilation and
> the grandeur of inspiration.*"
> —William Blake

The challenge-riddle of the "*Sun Gate*" is: "all that glitters is not gold." Just as surely as the sunlight can pierce the darkness, so too is it sometimes blinding to see what is right in front of us. We must be ready, always, not caught basking in the glowing rays of the shining sun. The apex of solar power at noon reflects the heights of empires and all systems—but these too must ebb and fall in their own cyclic tides. Everything is in motion; and everything everywhere is connected together.

It is from the "*Solar Gate*" that an initiate must

prepare in "self-honesty" for the forthcoming encounter with the "Annihilator" energies of *Nergal*.
This is the *Wall of Fire* confronted along the *Pathway*. After being given charged on the Mardukite
mystic path of the *"Ladder of Lights"* by *Nabu* at
the second gate, there are many Anunnaki figures
(representing lessons on the path) from those who
stood against the rise of a *Mardukite Babylon*—
Ishtar, *Shammash* and *Nergal*—all of which have
played a part in its abolition. Even *Shammash*
(UTU) sided with Dumuzi against Marduk in that
tablet cycle; and then later against *Nabu*, siding
with *Nergal* and *Ninurta* in what some scholars
call the "Pyramid Wars," which included mass-de-
struction of the ancient "Middle East," leaving a
resonant imprint of unrest forever on that locale.

"The Great Hymn of Shammash" is potentially the
most significant mystical cuneiform tablet tran-
scription from Mesopotamia regarding the *"sun-
god."* A seeker will see that it reveres more than
simply the "physical *sun*," but the "sublime light
of truth" personified by the Anunnaki position
held *Shammash* (*Uddu/Utu*). Several of the lines
(particularly at the beginning and end) on the tablet cycle have worn away, but the definitive academic version, first appearing in *"Babylonian Wisdom Literature"* by W. Lambert (in 1960), remains the most complete modern translation for
both mystics and scholars.

Any "moral dogma" presented reflects other Babylonian wisdom tablet series, such as "Book of the
Law of Marduk"—given as Mardukite *Tablet-L* in
our "*Anunnaki Bible*." The "*Great Hymn of Shammash*" reads:—

21. You climb to the mountains surveying the
    earth,
22. You suspend from the heavens the circle of
    the lands,
23. You care for all the peoples of the lands,
24. And everything that EA (*Enki*), king of the
    counselors had created is entrusted to you.
25. Whatever has breath you shepherd without
    exception,
26. You are keeper in upper and lower regions.
27. Regularly and without cease you traverse
    the heavens,
28. Every day you pass over the broad
    earth . . .
33. Shepherd of that beneath, keeper of that
    above,
34. You, *Shammash*, direct, you are the light of
    everything.
35. You never fail to cross the wide expanse of
    sea,
36. The depth of which the IGIGI know not.
37. *Shammash*, your glare reaches down to the
    abyss
38. So that monsters of the deep behold your
    light . . .

45. Among all the IGIGI there is none who toils but you,
46. None who is supreme like you in the whole pantheon of gods.
47. At your rising the gods of the land assemble,
48. Your fierce glare covers the land.
49. Of all the lands of varied speech,
50. You know their plans, you scan their way.
51. The whole of mankind bows to you,
52. *Shammash*, the universe longs for your light.
88. A man who covets his neighbor's wife
89. Will . . . before his appointed day.
90. A nasty snare is prepared for him . . .
91. Your weapon will strike at him, and there will be none to save him.
92. His father will not stand for his defense,
93. And at the judge's command his brothers will not plead.
94. He will be caught in a copper trap that he did not foresee.
95. You destroy the horns of a scheming villain,
96. A zealous . . . his foundations are undermined.
97. You give the unscrupulous judge experience fetters,
98. Him who accepts a present and yet lets justice miscarry, you make bear his

punishment.

99. As for him who declines a present but nevertheless takes the part of the weak,

100. It is pleasing to *Shammash*, and he will prolong his life . . .

124. The progeny of evil-doers will fail.

125. Those whose mouth says "No," their case is before you.

126. In a moment you discern what they say;

127. You hear and examine them; you determine the lawsuit of the wronged.

128. Every single person is entrusted to your hands;

129. You manage their omens; that which is perplexing you make plain.

130. You observe, *Shammash*, prayer, supplication, and benediction.

131. Obeisance, kneeling, ritual murmurs, and prostration.

132. The feeble man calls you from the hollow of his mouth,

133. The humble, the weak, the afflicted, the poor,

134. She whose son is captive constantly and unceasingly confronts you.

135. He whose family is remote, whose city is distant,

136. The shepherd amid the terror of the steppe confronts you,

137. The herdsman in warfare, the keeper of

sheep among enemies.

138. *Shammash*, there confronts you the caravan, those journeying in fear,

139. The traveling merchant, the agent who is carrying capital.

140. *Shammash* there confronts you the fisherman with his net,

141. The hunter, the bowman who drives the game,

142. With his bird net the fowler confronts you.

143. The prowling thief, the enemy of *Shammash*,

144. The marauder along the tracks of the steppe confronts you.

145. The roving dead, the vagrant soul,

146. They confront you, *Shammash*, and you hear all.

147. You do not obstruct those that confront you...

148. For my sake, *Shammash*, do not curse them!

149. You grant revelations, *Shammash*, to the families of men,

150. Your harsh face and fierce light you give to them . . .

154. The heavens are not enough as the vessel into which you gaze,

155. The sum of the lands is inadequate as a seer's bowl . . .

159. You deliver people surrounded by mighty waves,

160. In return you receive their pure, clear libations . . .

165. They in their reverence laud the mention of you,

166. And worship your majesty for ever . . .

174. Which are the mountains not clothed with your beams?

175. Which are the regions not warmed by the brightness of your light?

176. Brightener of gloom, Illuminator of darkness,

177. Dispeller of darkness, Illuminator of the broad earth . . .

Invoking the "solar force"—whether *Shammash* or by another name—is common not only within the mysticism of Sumer and Babylon, but throughout esoteric history. The name "*Samas*" is called upon no less than a dozen times throughout the "Maqlu Ritual"—(called "Maklu" in Simon's work) a ceremonial discourse and cuneiform tablet series catalogued as Mardukite *Liber-M* and *Tablet-M*. [Refer to "*Anunnaki Rites*" or "*The Maqlu Ritual Book*" edited by Joshua Free.]

In many instances from the *Maqlu* series, *Shammash* is called alongside *Marduk* to destroy the wickedness and evil-doers in the world. Although *Shammash* later sided against *Marduk*, the name is invoked in Mardukite literature of the "*Ladder of Lights*" (or "*Stairway to the Stars*"), following the original Babylonian ideal of "unification," even if only to maintain control of the entire Anunnaki pantheon under *Marduk*—just as we see with the inclusion of many other Anunnaki names in the Babylonian paradigm. The "Law-Code" attributed to *King Hammurabi*, is dedicated to a "divine" knowledge transmission from both *Shammash* and *Marduk*:—

> *By the command of Samas*
> *The Judge of Heaven and Earth,*
> *May truth and righteousness reign supreme*
> *Throughout the lands.*
> *Let those who read these words have a pure*
>   *heart*
> *And pray to Marduk, my Lord,*
> *And Sarpanit, my Lady, his consort.*
> *By the decree of Samas,*
> *I have been given my Eternal Legacy.*
> *If a forthcoming ruler should read my words*
> *And not corrupt the law,*
> *Then may Samas extend the length of his reign*
>   *on Earth,*
> *And he shall ever reign in righteousness over*
>   *his subjects.*

Mystical incantations for the "*Shammash Gate*" are strongly influenced by the previously given hymn. No prayer dedicated exclusively to *Shamm-*

ash (or the "sun-god") was found in the *Kuyunjik* collection. Instead, like the *Maqlu* series, the Babylonian invocations of that series are directed to both *Samas* and *Marduk*. One interesting example, however, is an incantation from "*Prayers of the Lifting of the Hand – Tablet 53,*" to be used "against the evils attending an eclipse of the moon." It is directed to EA (*Enki*), *Shammash* and *Marduk*. Leonard King offers the following description of the eclipse tablet:—

> "No. 53 (*K 3859* + *Sm. 383*) preserves the bottom portion of a tablet and contains a prayer to *Ia*, *Samas*, and *Marduk*, of which both the beginning and end are missing. The supplicant states that he is praying after an eclipse of the Moon and he implores these three deities to rescue him from the clutches of a spectre, by whom he is continually haunted. What remains of the *Obverse* commences as follows:—

O arbiter of the world, *Marduk*, the mighty, the lord of Itura!
   abkal kis-sa-ti ilu-Marduk sal-ba-[bu bil]
   I.TURRA

O EA, *Samas*, and *Marduk* deliver me,
   ilu-I-a ilu-Samas u ilu-Marduk ya-a-si ru-
   sa-nim-ma

And through your mercy let me come to
prosperity!
    ina an-ni-ku-nu i-sa-ru-tu lul-lik

O *Samas*, the spectre that striketh fear, that for
many days
    *ilu-Samas ikimmu mu-pal-li-hi sa is-tu u-mi
ma-'-du-ti*

Has been bound on my back, and is not loosed,
    arki-ya rak-su-ma la muppatiru(ru)

Through the whole hath . . . me, through the
whole night hath stricken me with terror!
    *ina kal u-mi iksus-an-ni ina kal musi up-ta-
na-lah-an-ni*

The supplicant then describes the ways in
which he is tormented by the spectre, who
defiles him and attacks his face, his eyes,
his back, his flesh and his whole body. On
the reverse of the tablet he recounts to
Samas how he has tried to appease and to
restrain his tormentor. Apparently his efforts have met with no success for he now
turns to the *Sun-god* for relief, which he
prays he may receive through his mighty
command that is not altered, and through
the command of *Marduk*, the arbiter of the
gods."

— 5 —

NERGAL & ERESHKIGAL :
"MARS" AND "THE SHADOWLANDS"

The legendary "*Underdark*" or "*Realm of the dead*" has been all too colorfully—or perhaps mono-chromatically—depicted by mythographers as merely a pile a rotting bodies, an infinite swamp, or with the arrival of dualism –a hellfire of intolerable damnation. Cuneiform tablet descriptions of the "*Shadowlands*"—or the "Great Below"—are indeed conceivably "darker" in the spectrum of mortal comprehension.

Traversing the Celestial Spheres on the "*Ladder of Lights,*" we are confronted with a "Dweller of the Threshold" to our "Dark Night of the Soul"—and ultimately a spiritual rebirth—rising as a phoenix; as a "*god,*" readied for access to the (next) "*Marduk Gate.*" Figures of the "*Underworld zonei*" play important functions and roles affecting human consciousness regarding death, entropy and physical cycles observed in the cosmos. Any "good" or "bad" is based strictly on human sentiment. The "*Kingdom of Shadows*"—access to its true knowledge and mystical interpretation of these energetic currents—has been shrouded in occult mystery for a very long time, and perhaps for good reason.

Where *Inanna-Ishtar* is "*goddess of love and war*" for the "upper realm," "realm of light (stars)," and "world of life," her *sister—Ereshkigal—*is so for the "lower realm," equated with the "*Underworld*" or "*Land of the Dead.*" She shares this domain with *Nergal*—the "death-god" or "plague-god"—archetypal "war-god" representing the *Martian* energy current. The word "KI.GAL" (as in "*Eresh-Ki-Gal*") is usually translated by scholars in academia as "*Great Below.*" This is a curious ascription when nearly all other cuneiform applications of the word "KI" (for "*Ki-Gal*") suggest a literal meaning: "Great Earth" or "Great Lands." The position-role and accepted lineage of Ereshkigal remains stable across most contemporary interpretations, but such is not the case with Nergal.

Nergal—the "*Great Watcher*"—(NER = "*Watcher,*" GAL = "*Great*") is something of an enigma on tablet sources. Early twentieth century scholars could not ascertain his parentage definitively. More importantly, the designation given to him of "eight" is not harmonious with the Base-60 system of Mesopotamian mathematics—where other Anunnaki designations are divisible by "60"—nor is *Ninib-Adad*, the Babylonian "storm-god" (also within this pantheon) who bares the number "four." This may be appropriate as the two deities are connected in the *Erra Epos* tablet cycle. However, the fact remains that: given the Sumerian ambiguity left to us from the available cuneiform sources, at best we can assume his father (or grandfather) is either *Enlil* or *Enki*. We only know for certain that *Nergal* is not directly the offspring of *Anu*. If he were, he would be listed higher in the pantheon. But, *Nergal* is too young for this ranking anyways.

Based on known Anunnaki marriage customs, it would be appropriate if *Nergal* were actually the love-child of *Enlil* and *Ninlil* as Samuel Kramer describes—

> "*Enlil*, (still) impersonating 'the man of the gate,' cohabits with her [*Ninlil*] and impregnates her. As a result *Ninlil* conceives *Meslam-taea*, more commonly known as *Nergal*."

In contrast, the late controversial Sumeriologist, Zecharia Sitchin, suggests *Enki* as *Nergal's* father in his genealogical accounts. This might be more plausible, making *Nergal* and *Ereshkigal* "half-siblings," in a similar manner found between *Marduk* and *Ishtar*. In this way, their union—an embodiment of "divine couple-hood,"—would have been "blessed" by the Anunnaki Assembly of "gods," much as a union of *Marduk* and *Ishtar* would have been. It is sometimes confusing because by standards of the "younger pantheon" and Mardukite tradition, *Enki* is practically everyone's "*Father*"— the one they all go to regardless of their parenting lineage.

Enki plays a very fatherly for *Ereshkigal* during one of the earliest Sumerian tablet cycles, describing primordial creation—when she is carried off to *Kutha* or the *"Underworld"* by the serpent-monster, KUR. Of all the *"Elder Gods,"* it is *Enki* that goes after her—though she is later made *"Queen of the Underworld"* and allowed to remain there. By this account, *Enki* is the first of very few who ever "descend" to the realm of the "dead" and able to return permanently [*"resurrected"*] from that state— the others being primarily *Ishtar* and *Marduk*—in recorded epics.

Modern traditions observe *Ereshkigal* as an archetypal *"Dragon Queen of the Netherworld,"* ruling with her dark king, *Nergal.* [Their courtship is described on the Mardukite *Tablet-U* series.] In some interpretations, she replaces the KUR-current (position) for Babylonian mythography; and she is given domain over seven Egyptian-Osirian *"death-gates,"* fluently described in both Egyptian sources and the *Inanna-Ishtar* tablet cycle of *"Descent to the Underworld."* She is given a role of high esteem by the "seven" Anunnaki Judges, encountering every dead spirit to pass through the gates. Egyptologist, E.A. Budge, weighs in, explaining:—

"After the spirit had appeared before *Ereshkigal*, it seems that the *Anunnaki* sat in judgment upon it, and with *Mammitu,*

the goddess of the destinies of men, pro-
ceeded to discuss the good and evil deeds
that it had done in the body."

There are some colorful accounts that demonstrate
that Nergal also moves back and forth across the
"*Underworld Gates*" acting as an "*angel of
death*"—the *Ares/Mars* "god of destruction" in the
pantheon. It should be understood that in mythology, the energy current represents radioactive
decay and entropic destruction and not a spiritual
idea of "death."

The two "*Shadowland*" rulers have quite the col-
laborative enterprise with one half acting as a
"Great Destroyer" and the other half burying the
dead. Though not a Christian-like Hell or sicken-
ing Hades, the Shadowlands represent the Anunnaki "death-machine" that seals the entire circuitry
of humanity.

The lore reveals the Anunnaki as
Guardians and *Gatekeepers* of both
"Life" and "Death" for humans in
this "Earthly" physical existence.

Nergal is also known as ENGIDUDU ("*Lord who
prowls by night*")—commander of the "*Sebittu,*"
the famous *Seven Demons* of the Anunnaki—used
for dealing out plagues and pestilence. This is
hardly portrayed as "evil"; originally presented as
a means for gods to maintain "balance" on Earth.

"Left-hand" traditions emphasize the *Sebittu* and *Nergal* unnecessarily. Another Semitic "Angel of Death"—*Azazel*—comes from a "realm of light" —like *Shammash*, *Nergal's* counterpart on the *Erra Epos* tablet cycle describing politics and destruction of the ancient "Middle East."

As a "war god," *Nergal* is invoked pre-combat for military blessings. The Babylonian example which follows is derived from the German anthology titled *"Ritualtafeln,"* transcribed by R. Campbell Thomson in his *"Semitic Magic"*:—

> *Ritual: when an enemy [attacks] the king and*
> * his land . . .*
> *The king shall go forth on the right wing of the*
> * army,*
> *And thou shalt sweep the earth clean,*
> * and sprinkle pure water,*
> *And set [three] altars, one for Ishtar, one for*
> *Shammash,*
> *And one for Nergal,*
> *And offer each a loaf of wheaten meal (flour),*
> *And make a mash of honey and butter,*
> *Pouring in dates and . . .-meal,*
> *And sacrifice three full-grown sheep,*
> *Flesh of the right thigh, hinsa-flesh and*
> * sume-flesh thou shalt offer,*
> *Sprinkle upuntu with cypress on a censer,*
> *And make a libation of honey, butter, wine, oil*
> * and scented oil,*

Then shalt thou make an image of the foe in
*   tallow,*
Bend backwards his face with a cord;
The . . . of the king, who is named like his
*   master,*
Shall . . . the robes of the king . . .
Shall stand before the preparation and
*   repeat this formula before Shammash. . .*

Nergal was never "officially" known as *Erra* in
Sumer. The *Erra Epos* tablet cycle (also known as
"*Erra and Isum*" and given in the present anthology as Mardukite *Tablet-V* series) is of Akkadian
origin. The epithet "*Erra*" is a somewhat derogat-
ory name for *Nergal*—a corruption of the names
he did possess: *Irrigal* or *Erakal*—with "*Erra*"
now meaning a "Servant of Ra" (*Marduk*), which
he clearly was not. Contemporary translators attribute authorship of this epic to the pen of *Kab-
ti-Ilani-Marduk*—a scribe-priest or priest-king related to a 12th Century B.C. "Babylonian Reformation" led by *Marduk-Kabit-Aheshu* according to
cuneiform King-Lists.

The account follows:—*Marduk* gives a warning
prophecy about the devastation that will ultimately
result if he were to step down from his seat at
Babylon. This prediction is nothing short of "apo-
calyptic," describing the ruin of Babylon and all of
the great Mesopotamian cities. *Nergal* goes to
Babylon and explains to *Marduk* that his "self-

made" supremacy has angered the other (Anunnaki) gods, and that *Marduk* is in possession of something (a mysterious object never clearly defined) that not only "powers" or "empowers" Babylon, but all of the other Mesopotamian cities of the gods as well. When *Marduk* cannot be convinced to leave "his seat" in Babylon, *Nergal* attempts a different tactic by describing various other "holy artifacts" that would ensure his righteous rule. These objects happen to all be in the "*Shadowlands*" and would require retrieval by *Marduk* personally. *Nergal* promises to "watch over" Babylon while *Marduk* is gone and promises very distinctly that nothing will "change" during his absence.

The tablets are obscure about the actual nature of the "holy artifacts" *Marduk* goes in search for, or the "object of power" propelling Babylon (kept in a secret room called the *gigunu* that adjoined Marduk's throne chamber at the top of his ziggurat-temple). But we know that the "object of power" was disturbed by *Nergal* as soon as *Marduk* "left his seat" in pursuit of the "holy artifacts." Instantly, the "waters stopped flowing," first in Babylon, then in the remaining great cities. The power and strength of ancient Babylon had been weakened, but not yet destroyed. Its destruction came later—a planned attack resulting from mistaken blame for this tragedy, all of which was placed on *Marduk*.

When the "Supernal Trinity" called an "Anunnaki Assembly" of gods regarding the incident, all of the "younger pantheon"—*Ninurta, Nergal, Shammash, Adar* and *Ishtar*—conspired in judgment against *Marduk* and *Nabu*, placing full blame on them for the collapse of the systems. Any *unity* of the "celestial pantheon" was split forever. And with *Marduk* absent in pursuit of the "holy artifacts," *Nabu* stood alone to face the entire assembly, as translated by Zecharia Sitchin:—

> Speaking for his father, *Nabu* blamed *Ninurta*, and revived old accusations against *Nergal* in regard to the disappearance of the pre-Diluvial monitoring instruments and failure to prevent sacrilege in Babylon [referring to the disturbance of the "power object"]; he got into a shouting match with *Nergal*, and showing disrespect:
> *Nabu* to *Enlil*, evil he spoke:
> "There is no justice!
> Destruction was conceived!
> *Enlil* against Babylon caused evil to be planned!"
> It was an unheard of accusation against the Lord of the Command.
> *Enki* spoke up, but it was in defense of his son, not of *Enlil*.
> Asked *Enki*:
> "What are Marduk and Nabu actually accused of?"

His eye was directed especially at his son
Nergal:
"Why do you continue the opposition?"

After the council assembly agrees that *Marduk*
should be removed from power in Babylon, *Nergal* and *Ninurta* decide to wage an entire nuclear
war against Babylon and the *"Tribes of Nabu."*
Many lamentation tablets were behind from the
wake of this. More devastating than the descriptions of fiery blasts themselves were the accounts
of "evil winds" turning entire cities into ghost-
towns. Traditions of *Marduk* and *Nabu* were
moved underground and to Egypt where *Marduk*
already had established a new civilization of followers, presenting himself as *"Amon-Ra"*—*"The
Unseen God."* Devastation in the "Middle East"
left its inhabitants and all surrounding-area tribes
hostile toward one another—persisting to the
present day, a war that has been waging on point-
lessly for thousands of years.

* * *

It is easy, then, to understand how *Nergal* became
the prototype of the *Mars-Ares* personage. As the
word *"Erra"* evolved, it later came to denote *Nergal* as the "Annihilator," a role previously given in
Sumerian literature to GI.BIL—GIRRA or *"fires
of god."* *Nergal* and *Shammash* frequently employ
these *"fires of god"* to carry out judgments decreed

by the Anunnaki Assembly. Nergal is even de-scribed in the *Gilgamesh* cycle as "the ambusher who spares no one." The challenge of the "*Mars Gate*" regarding initiation on Mystical Path is thus the temperance of anger, pride, &tc.—overcoming *all Fear*—destructive energies that will manifest within the initiate uncontrollably chaotic if al-lowed to pass through the (next) "*Marduk Gate*."

Modern mystical and astral experiences with "*Un-derworld*" currents reveal these "*Shadowland*" beings as often pale or with blue-hued skin and dark or white hair (sometimes long or unkempt). The absence of clothing also seems prominent in the Underworld, particularly among females. This is best depicted in mental imagery conjured of two "naked goddesses"—*Ereshkigal* and *Ishtar*—fam-ously confronting one another in physical rivalry, sprawling across the floors of the "*Underworld*" palace (as described in the "Descent" tablet cycle).

The invocation of the "*Nergal Gate*" used by mod-ern Mardukites—given within the Mardukite *Tablet-B* series of "*The Complete Anunnaki Bible*"—is strongly influenced by the twenty-sev-enth tablet in the "*Prayers of the Lifting of the Hand*" series from the *Kuyunjik* collection. Ac-cording to translator, L. W. King, the tablet was originally in possession of *King Ashurbanipal*, so the original inscription bore his name as the bene-factor of the prayer's blessings. In this instance, the prayer actually invokes *Nergal* as the "first-born of *Nunamnir*," who is *Enlil*. The prayer is as follows:

I mighty lord, hero, first-born of *Nunamnir*!
siptu bi-lum gas-ru ti-iz-ka-[ru bu-kur ilu-NU.NAM.NIR]

Prince of the Anunnaki, lord of the battle!
a-sa-rid ilu-A-nun-na-[ki bil tam-ha-ri]

Offspring of Kutusar, the mighty queen!
i-lit-ti ilu-KU.TU.SAR [sar-ra-tum rabitum(tum)]

O *Nirgal*, strong one of the gods, the darling of Ninminna!
ilu-Nirgal kas-kas ilani [na-ram ilu-NIN.MIN.NA]

Thou treadest in the bright heavens, lofty is thy place!
su-pa-ta ina sami-i illuti [sa-ku man-za-az-ka]

Thou art exalted in the Underworld and art the benefactor of its . . .
ra-ba-ta ina aralli-[ma asira(ra) LA.TI-su]

With EA among the multitudes of the gods inscribe thy counsel,
it-ti ilu-I.A. ina puhur [ilani mi-lik-ka su-tur]

With SIN [*Nanna*] in the heavens, you seek all things,

it-ti ilu-SIN ina sami-i [ta-si gim-ri]

And BIL [*Bel*], thy father has granted thee that
the dark-headed race, all living creatures,
*id-din-ka-ma ilu-BIL abu-[ka sal-mat
kakkadu puhur napisti(ti)]*

The cattle of *Nirgal*, created things, thy hand
should rule!
*bu-ul ilu-NIRGAL nam-mas-[si-i ka-tuk-ka
ip-kid]*

I, so and so, the son of so and so, am thy
servant!
ana-ku pulanu apil pulani [arad-ka]

The . . . of god and goddess are laid upon me!
mi-lat ili u ilu-istari [is-sak-nu-nim-ma]

Uprooting and destruction are my house!
nasahu u hu-lu-uk-ku-[u basu-u ina biti-ya]

[. . .] (untranslated)
ka-bu-u IA si-mu-[u it-tal-pu-nin-ni]

Since thou are beneficent, I have turned to thy
divinity!
*as-sum gam-ma-la-ta bi-li [as-sa-har ilu-ut-
ka]*

Since thou are compassionate, I have sought
for thee!
as-sum ta-ai-ra-ta [is-ti-'-u-ka]

Since thou are empathic, I have beheld . . .
as-sum mu-up-pal-sa-ta [a-ra-mar . . .]

Since thou are merciful, I have taken my stand before thee!
as-sum ri-mi-ni-ta [at-ta-ziz pani-ka]

Truly pity me and hearken to my cries!
ki-nis naplis-an-ni-ma [si-mi ka-ba-ai]

May thine angry heart have rest!
ag-gu lib-ba-ka [li-nu-ha]

Loosen my sin, my offense . . .
[pu]-tur an-ni hi-[ti-ti . . .]

[. . .] (untranslated / broken)
. . . -sir lib-bi ilu-ti-ka . . .

I god and angry goddess . . .
ilu u ilu-istaru zi-nu-ti sab- . . .

Let me talk of thy greatness, Let me bow in humility before thee!
nir-bi-ka lu-uk-bi [da-li-li-ka lud-lul]

— 6 —

MARDUK : "KING OF THE GODS"

Ancient Mesopotamia witnessed a rise of the "younger pantheon," which took great interest in the activities and devotion of humans on earth. Of them, perhaps the most famous for "planetary mythology" is *Marduk—Jupiter*—the national god of Babylon. Much like his half-sister—*Inanna-Ishtar*—a self-made "queen of the heavens," Marduk exploited his own personal conviction, cunning and tenacity to secure his position as the primary controller of the "*Ladder of Lights*"—the BAB.ILI, "Gates of the Gods"—even exceeding the position of his father—*Enki*—by assuming the role and functions of *Enlil*—the *Anu* of "Material Existence"—to his followers.

Little mention of *Marduk* is actually made in earlier pre-Babylonian Sumerian cuneiform literature (under any name or epithet). He was content, for a time, to remain an assistant to *Enki*, mastering the esoteric arts of "magic" and "science" in *Eridu*. *Marduk* was originally given the numeric designation of "10" and told to "wait his turn"—at the "*Age of Aries*"—to rise in the pantheon. His most familiar name—MARDUK—is actually an evolved transliteration derived from the Semitic "*meridug*" (*Merodach*). An older version of his name is written: AMAR.UTU (*a.mar-utu.ki* = "Light of the

Sun on Earth")—often interpreted by contemporary scholars as *"solar calf"* or *"son of the sun."*
This provides some background to *Marduk's* esteem. And as the foremost son of *Enki*, he gained power quickly.

The later Semitic name *"Maerdechai"* or *"Mordechai"* came from the name of *Marduk* in Chaldeo-Babylonian language—*"silik-mul.u-khi"*—meaning *"Marduk is God."* The more commonly used MAR.DUG means *"son of the pure mound"*—thought to be a reference to pyramids not only in Mesopotamia, but also in Egypt, where he raised himself as the leader of a third party (interpretation) of Anunnaki gods—the Egyptian Pantheon—as *"Amon-Ra,"* again identifying himself with the "solar" current and "stars" directly.

Marduk's decision to raise himself to a monotheistic-like *"God"* status in Babylon created new political issues for the other Anunnaki on Earth. Exercising his "divine rights" stretched tensions between lineages—of *Enki* and *Enlil*—for supremacy on earth. When *Marduk* and *Ishtar* did not partner for this role, each sought the right to install their own dynastic lineages and choose the humans as "Kings" in their stead, during the "Age of Aries," beginning in 2160 B.C.—the birth of a New Dynastic global era. Zecharia Sitchin explains how in Babylon:—

> "*Marduk* was proclaimed King of the
> Gods, replacing *Enlil*, and the other gods
> were required to pledge allegiance to him
> and to come to reside in Babylon where
> their activities could be easily supervised.
> This usurpation of Enlilship was accom-
> panied by an extensive Babylonian effort
> to forge the ancient texts. The most import-
> ant texts were rewritten and altered so as to
> make *Marduk* appear as the Lord of the
> Heavens, the Creator. . ."

Certainly, the other Anunnaki were less than ap-
preciative of *Marduk's* desire to rule over them.
Yet throughout the *"Age of Aries,"*—his time to
reign—he was not left to his own accord in
Babylon (or in Egypt). This seems to have been a
disciplinarian act by the other gods.

If we take the most literal interpretations at face
value, *Marduk* lost all rights of kingship "in heav-
en" when he took a "human" wife instead of his
betrothed half-sister. His argument was that his
consort—*Sarpanit*—was a descendent of *Adapa*,
and thus of Anunnaki bloodline via *Enki*; that
Ishtar was no more interested in the union than he
was, and it had not affected her rise to power; and
finally, if not "in heaven," why not "on earth"?
The logic seems to have gone unheard and where
the "Mardukite" legacy was threatened in Babylon
and Egypt, as its survival was frequently aided by

"foreign hands."

In post-Sumerian Assyrian accounts, *Marduk*—as the great "father-god" ASSUR or ASHUR ("*Ashshur*")—seems to emerge in their tradition as if from nowhere. This led some scholars in the late-1800's and early-1900's to wonder if *Marduk* was a purely fictitious figure imagined into being for solely political reasons. Similarly, while *Sarpanit*—also *Sarapan* or *Zarpanitu*—is mentioned often in Babylonian prayer-tablets, she does not appear in any significant mythic tablet (saga) cycles. Her elevated status is rightly achieved due to her direct relationship with *Marduk*, and together, they are the parents of *Nabu*.

At the spring equinox "A.KI.TI" festival, *Sarpanit* is the "spring-maiden" of fertility ceremonies in Babylon. In the "*Edaphic Tradition*" that spread across Europe, she is known as "*Erua,*" or more appropriately, ERU. Later European "elven-faerie-dragon" dynasties (explored elsewhere in *Liber-D "Elvenomcon"* by Joshua Free) claimed descent from *Marduk* and *Sarpanit*, their "star-goddess mother of vegetation and fertility." And sure enough "*Eru*" is an Akkadian word for "pregnancy."

* * *

For nearly two millennium, *Marduk* and *Sarpanit* are national patrons of all priest-magicians and priestesses of Babylonia. In fact, by literal title, "Babylon" became the *"seat of the gods,"* but by Mardukite standards, this was to be realized differently than either *monotheism* or *polytheism*. The system of myth and magic born in Babylon was first and foremost dedicated to *Marduk's "Divine World Order,"* often illustrated through the first mystical *"kabbalah"* system: *10 gates, 2 doors* and *7 levels*—just like the design for the Mardukite ziggurat "E.TEMEN. AN.KI"—*"The Temple of Heaven and Earth."*

An excellent incantation-tablet example invokes *Marduk* and *Sarpanit* after an experience of "evil from an eclipse," as first excavated by the French and transliterated in Vincent Scheil's *"Une Saison de Fouilles a Sippar,"* later translated by Thomson, who explains to us in *"Semitic Magic"* that the prayer was given to *King Assurbanipal* by his brother, *Samas-sumukin.*

Both scholarly sources were used to reconstruct the full prayer in tact with both *English* and *French* translations of the original *Cuneifom* transliteration:—

  . . . O great lady, kindly mother,
    FR. ôo grande déesse, mère miséricordieuse
      C. *beltu sa-qu-ti ummu rim-ni-ti*

  Amid the many stars of heaven,
    FR. parmi les nomlbreuses étoiles clu ciel

C. *ina ma'-du-ti kakkabe sa-ma-mi*

Thou art mistress . . .
  FR. vous êtes reine . . .
    C. *beltu ka-a-si* . . .

I, *Samas-sum-ukin*, the king, servant of his god
  FR. moi *Samas* sum ukîn roi, serviteur de
  son dieu
    C. *ana-ku Samas sum ukin sarru, GAL ili-su*

Vicegerent of his god *Marduk* and his goddess
  Sarpanit
  FR. vicaire de son dieu *Marduk* et de sa déesse
    Zarpanitum,
    C. *sakin ili-su (ilu)-Marduk (ilu)-Istarti-su
      (ilu)-Zar-pa-ni-tum*

Of the evils of the eclipse of the moon, Fixed for
  the fifteenth day of Shebat
  FR. des maux de l'éclipse de lune fixée au 15
    du mois d'AB
    C. *ana lumun AN-MI (ilu)-Sin sa ina arhi AS
      um 15 (kam) sak-nu*

Of the evils of the signs and omens, evil,
  baneful,
  FR. des maux de signes et visions funestes,
    malfaisantes
    C. *ana lumun idati SI-BIT-mes limnuti la
      tabuti*

Which have occurred in my palace and my land
  FR. qui arriveraient dans mon palais et mon

pays,
   C. *sa ina e-kal-ya (MU) u mati-ya ibba-su*

I am afraid, and I fear, and I tremble
   FR. j'ai peur, je tremble, je frémis
     C. *pal-ha-ku-ma ad-ra-ku u su-ta-du-ra-ku*

Let not these evils draw near to me or my house
   FR. ces maux, de moi et de ma maison
     C. *lumnu suatu ya-a-si u biti-ya*

[. . .] "Let them not approach [come near]"
   FR. qu'ils n'approchent pas
     C. *a-a TE*

Accept the *upuntu*-plant from me and receive
   my prayer.
   FR. agrée l'tpuntu, agrée ma prière
     C. *upuntu muh-ri-in-ni-ma li-ki-e un-ni-ni*

What becomes apparent when researching Mardukite-specific materials: Marduk is the original "rebel-god," rising to supremacy and places himself in the highest positions—"Primordial Dragonslayer" and "Creator of the Universe"—*Jupiter*—the great force that maintains the orderly zones of the "solar system." His domain evolves to include all sciences and magics—the true understanding of the hidden patterns and secret doctrines of the cosmos. It is here that all magical traditions were born—later fragmented into systems practiced throughout human history, and all based in symbols and signs, names and numbers, prayers and incantations. These are the esoteric or "*Hermetic*" arts first known to *Enki*, then *Marduk*, and finally *Nabu*. The challenge of the "*Marduk Gate*" is then to actually apply the esoteric formulas of "Cosmic Law" to direct and channel the powers of the Universe toward causal manifestations in creation and personal ascension—otherwise true "*magic*." Editor Simon relays in his handbook:—

> "Where *Nergal* represents Will—pure Will, unassuaged by purpose—and *Inanna*, desire; *Marduk* is the Law. This Law is no so much the Law of courts and decrees, but the Law of science, the lineaments of the created universe. Through the first five Gates we have become initiated into the use and sense of various Forces; in the *Sixth Gate* we become masters at manipulating all of them, at mixing them to produce various effects."

Mardukite "initiates" actually invoke this current in numerous ways. However, in maintaining consistency with our current volume, it is the incantation-prayer tablets we are most interested, and there are many. Several "prayers" to *Marduk* may be found in throughout this "complete anthology." Traditional "Gate Invocations" generally follow the formula demonstrated in the key examples from the *Kuyunjik* collection that the current editor has chosen to adapt for this series.

The "*Isagila*" mentioned in its text is a reference to *Marduk's* primary ziggurat-temple in Babylon, also transliterated: E.SAG.ILU or *Esaggadhu*.

> *Siptu gaasru supuuu iziz Assur*
> Almighty, powerful and strong one of *Assur.*

> *Rubu tiizkaru bukur NU.DIM.MUD*
> Exalted, noble-blood, firstborn of *Enki.*

> *Marduk salbabu muris I.TUR.RA*
> Almighty *Marduk*, who causes the *Itura* to rejoice.

> *Bil I.SAG.ILA tukultiti Babiliki raim I.ZID.DA*
> Lord of the *Isagila*, Aid to Babylon, Lover of the *Izida (E.ZIDA)*

> *Musalim napistiti asarid I.MAH.TIL.LA mudussuubalatu*
> Preserver of Life, Prince of *Imahtilla*, Renewer of Life.

> *Zulul maati gamil nisi rapsaati*
> Shadow over the Land, Protector of foreign lands.

> *Usumugal kalis parakkani*
> Forever is [*Marduk*] the Sovereign of Shrines.

> *Sumuka kalis ina pi nisi taaab*
> Forever is [*Marduk*] the name in the mouth of the people.

170

Marduk bilu rabuu ina kibitka kabitti luublut
Almighty *Lord Marduk* at your command I
remain alive.

Ina kibitika sirti luublut luuslimma
At your command let me live, let me be
perfect, let me behold your Divinity.

Luustammar iluutka
What I will to be, let me obtain my wishes.

Ima usaammaru luuksuud
[*Marduk*], cause righteousness to come from
my mouth.

Supsika damiktimtim inalibbiya
[*Marduk*], cause mercy to dwell in my heart.

Tiru u naanzazu likbuu damiktimtim
Return to Earth, establish yourselves and
command mercy.

Iliya liizziz ina imniya
May my god stand at my right hand.

Istariya liizziz ina sumiliya
May my goddess stand at my left hand.

Iliya sallimu ina idiya luukaaian
May my god who is favorable to the stars,
stand firmly at my side.

Surgamma kabaa simaa u magara
To speak the Word of Command, to hear my
prayer and show favor.

Amat akabbuu ima akabbuu luu maagrat
   When I speak, let the words by powerful.

Marduk bilu rabuu napistimtim kibi
   Almighty *Lord Marduk*, come and
      command life.

Balat napistiya kibi
   As you command my Life

Maharka namris adalluka luusbi
   Before you I bow, let me be satisfied

Bil urrula Ia litiska
   Bel's Fires go with you, *Ia* [*Enki*] smile
      upon you

Ilani sa kissati likrubuka
   May the Earth Gods be favorable to thee
      and me

Ilani rabuti libbaka litibu
   May the Good Gods delight in your mercy.

This incantation tablet continues on its reverse
with part of a prayer addressing Sarpanit as the:

   Queen of *Isagila*, the palace of the gods, the...
      mountain
      sar-rat I.SAG.ILA ikal ilani sa-du-u- . . .

   Lady of Babylon, the Shadow of lands!
      Bi-lit Babili-ki su-lul ma-ta-a-ti

   Lady of the gods, who loves to give life,
      ilu-Bilit ili sa bul-lu-ta i-ram-mu

Who gives succor in sorrow and distress,
  it-ti-rat ina puski u dannati

The . . . one, who holds the hand of . . .
  . . . *-ma-li-tu sa-bi-ta kata-du na-as-ki*

Who supports the weak, who pours out seed,
  i-pi-rat in-si sa-pi-kat ziru

Who protects life, who gives offspring
  and seed,
  na-si-rat napisti(ti) nadnat(at) aplu u ziru

Who bestows life, who takes away sighing,
  who accepts prayer,
  *ka-i-sat balatu li-kat un-ni-ni ma-hi-rat tas-
  lit*

Who has made the people, the whole of
  creation!
  ba-na-at nisi gi-mir nab-ni-ta

— 7 —

NINIB-NINURTA :
"WHO COMPLETES THE FOUNDATION"

Drawing from more readily available 19th Century "Assyriological" research, Simon's *"Necronomicon"* from the 1970's describes the Guardian of the *"Seventh Gate"* as the "youngest son" of *Enlil*. The name given is *Adar*, coupled with a footnote that the force is sometimes called *Ninib*. The remaining description is actually of a "storm-god" (not *Saturn*) and immediately the name *Adad* comes to mind—the "storm god" and "youngest son" of *Enlil* according to Sumerian tradition. So... Perhaps the author has made a mistake—some kind of typo. And what a critical point to have such obscurity: when we are on the brink of the final gate before reaching communion with the IGIGI—the *"Outer Ones."* Even many of the original Mardukite researchers misappropriated this energy current to *Adad-Ishkur* or *Ramman*—the "windstorm deity." This has been officially corrected in our archives.

As it turns out, ambiguity of ancient "Mardukite" records was not an oversight. The personage of *Ninib-Adar* is intentionally minimized for the Babylonian system. Confusing the "youngest son" of *Enlil* with his "oldest son"—born to half-sister *Ninhursag* or *Ninmah*—kept political attention away from any claims to "Enlilite" supremacy in Babylon. In Babylon, *Marduk* was unquestionably supreme—any access to a further "*Seventh Gate*" would require *his* direct assistance. In *short—Adar* is not a typo of *Adad*, but is in fact the *Assyrian* (and in some cases, *Akkadian*) name derived from *Nindar* or *Ninurta*—Anunnaki heir of *Enlil* and representation of *Saturn* in Sumerian tradition.

Superseding all previous esoteric regards, it is *Ninurta* who is selected by the Sumerian Anunnaki to give watch of the "*Saturn Gate*." Clearly this provided inspiration for *Marduk* to assume the "*Fifty Names*"—all the "Keys to the Kingdom"—under his name. Modern occult "self-initiates" of the earlier "Simon" work are aware that passing the "*Marduk Gate*" allows a magician-priest of the "Mardukite" tradition access to the *Fifty Names*—meaning direct access to the "*Arts of Civilization*" and "*Secret Formulas of the Cosmos*" [See "*The Tablets of Destiny*" by Joshua Free.] Most "New Age" Seekers are concerned with little else. For most who are diligent enough to seriously work through the gate-system, their work "Self-Honestly" ends here. Those who may have thought they had completed some type of "Ascension" journey through "*Star-Gates of the Anunnaki*" or "*Traversing the Seven Spheres*" using virtually all previously available lore, now discover they did not.

Naturally, very few modern practitioners have achieved "True Enlightenment" and useful "cognitions" via a Mesopotamian revival of any kind when using materials other than what is available exclusively from the *Mardukite Research Organization*.

Without the "Mardukite" foundation, other revivals become fanciful and imaginative reenactments that elevate consciousness to the same extent as any cultural-motif "New Age" creative visualization exercise. *Marduk* makes *himself* the "final gate" of the material systems without actually being so. And those who *do* pass on from the "*Marduk Gate*" do not always even reach Ninurta—*Saturn*—withholding, in part, a complete spiritual progression all due to a political "cover-up" in Babylon, concealing any knowledge of *Ninurta* as the Sumerian heir to *Enlilship* of the local system.

To understand the ambiguity, one must realize that *Ninurta* does not even originally appear in the Sumerian "Olympian" *Pantheon of Twelve* and it seems his position among the "younger pantheon" on the "*Ladder of Lights*" is jumbled for later "Mardukite" followers. We must assume this was to prevent Sumerian succession from in any way "stealing the spotlight" from the position of *Marduk*. Regarding the original Sumerian status of *Ninurta* and his absence from the pantheon, Zecharia Sitchin explains:—

"*Ninurta* was assigned the number 50, like his father. In other words, his dynastic rank was conveyed in a cryptographic message: If *Enlil* goes, you, *Ninurta*, step into his shoes; but until then, you are not one of the twelve, for the rank of '50' is occupied."

Among various excavated Sumerian tablet-cycles of KUR, the hero (or heroine) is attributed to one of three different characters—*Enki*, *Inanna* and *Ninurta*—each encountering the force differently. The epic concerning *Ninurta* is possibly the oldest most accurate epic from before Babylon, showing striking resemblances to later Babylonian revisions (of the "*Enuma Elis*") detailing *Marduk* as the serpent-slayer next in line for "*Enlilship.*" Loss of these details unfortunately led a broken spiritual system wrapped in Anunnaki politics. This is resolved in consciousness with a self-honest unification of the pantheon with "new" modern Mardukite standards of viewing the "younger generation" of Anunnaki gods. Doing this repairs a broken religio-magical system (or "spiritual paradigm"), now accessible to modern practitioners, scholars and esotericists for the very first time, *ever*—in a clarity not even known in the ancient world.

* * *

Ninurta is a hunter, but as a son of *Enlil* we should not be surprised to find him described also as a "plough-man" or "farmer god." Many from the Enlilite lineage are connected to agriculture and "farming," much as the lineage of *Enki* carries affinity for animals and "shepherding." In later Semtic lore, *Ninurta* appears as *Nimrod* (although this character is sometimes confused with *Nabu*), sharing the same role as in older appearances from Mesopotamian literature—assisting in the reformation of civilization after the *Flood*.

Politics enter the arena only when matters turn towards Babylon—*Ninurta* is actually the original organizer of Enlilite tribes against the Mardukites in Babylon. In one famous cuneiform epic, he is given the epithet "*Ishum*"—from the "*Erra Epos*" cuneiform tablet cycle ("*Erra and Ishum*") described in a prior chapter—meaning "scorcher." He acts as an adviser to *Nergal* (*Erra*) during the violent acts to "unseat" *Marduk* from Babylon.

Both *Ninurta* and his consort—*Bau* (or *Gula*)—are actually attributed healing properties in the original Sumerian mystical tradition. As the defeater of both "*Asag*" (or KUR) and ANZU (in another epic), *Ninurta* is called upon to "*defeat*" demons and "evil spirits"—of sickness and disease. *Bau*, especially, is a patron to nurses and doctors. At first glance, these attributes seem out of character as representations of the *Saturn*-current—which reflects a confrontation of the darkest ("hidden") parts of *ourselves* in combination with the final constraints of "Cosmic Law" as it applies to the local material system. The "absolute healing" seems more appropriate when we consider that the "*Saturn Gate*" is the final threshold crossing or barrier to "Ascension"—*liberation* from the material program—and its primary gatekeeper according to the Sumerian tradition, is *Ninurta*, the Anunnaki-decreed rightful heir to *Enlil*. The very essence of a "*seven-fold*" system comes into logic focus more clearly than ever before—the "*Foundation of Heaven and Earth*" is complete and the mysteries of the ziggurat "Temple of the Seven Spheres" are laid out before the Seeker.

The "*Seventh Gate*" leads to the "*Supernal Trinity*" of Anunnaki—the "*outer limits*" of our local system—a position in which *Ninurta* is waiting for heir-ship of in the Sumerian system. This means by some standard, era or version: *Enlil*, *Ninurta* and *Marduk* all maintain the designation (position) of "50." The heart of this beats a difficult fact to accept for the bloodline of *Marduk* and all those calling *Enki*, "Father" in the *Mardukite* paradigm. All this may seem trite to the uninitiated, but it is probably the deepest darkest kept secret in ancient Babylon—thus, even there deserving of the designation of *Saturn*. Proper realization of the system is what esotericists seek as the "*Hidden Key to the Necronomicon*." It not only brings harmony to the system for a modern practitioner—divine-messengers and temple-servants of the gods—but, for the gods *themselves*.

Mysteries of the "*Seventh Gate*" represent the highest initiation accessible to priests and priestesses *on earth*. More or less "divisions" of the whole does not change the whole. Others have simply broken down perceived fragments of reality into other *quantities*—the Babylonian "Gatesystem" consists of *seven*. The "Secrets of the Gates" are hidden throughout Babylon in mythic sagas and esoteric traditions of *Elder Gods* and the *younger pantheon* in Mesopotamia.

On many levels of manifestation, the "Gates" *are* functional. The "*Hidden Key*"—the paradigm represented by the whole—was essentially the *first* "government-secret" kept by priests and scribes occupying the highest positions—the final "combination sequence" to make the "Star Gate of Babylon" actually *work*.

Even as the "Seat" of *Marduk*, by Sumerian standards, the existence of Babylon and *Marduk's* "StarGate" was deemed "illegal" in Enlilite territory. Babylon was eventually destroyed—hence our misunderstood genetic memory of the "*Tower of Babylon*" incident. *Ninurta* held residence in several ancient Mesopotamian cities, but most scholars agree his primary ziggurat-temple was the *E.Shumedu* in Nippur.

Ninurta—as heir to *Enlil*—was a "solar deity" representing *Saturn*, but also *Sirius* in the old Sumerian astrology, as did *Marduk* later. *Sirius* is often referred to in mystical literature as the "sun behind the sun," and is considered the true and secret form of ancient "solar-worship." *Marduk* sought to represent the same "sun behind the sun" in Egypt. As one cannot see a candle flame when placed in front of the sun—the elusive celestial force of *Sirius* is shared as "Saturn of Stars," and part of a gateway or bridge beyond our system.

There is an excellent invocation to *Ninurta* elsewhere within the *Tablet-W* series, available in "*The Complete Book of Marduk*" and "*The Complete Anunnaki Bible.*" Prior to these developments, the original "Invocation of the Saturn Gate" (dedicated to *Ninurta*) used by modern Mardukite Chamberlains is also found in "*The Complete Anunnaki Bible.*" But another incantation example for esoteric experimentation or general research is included here, adapted from the second tablet of the "Prayers of the Lifting of the Hand" series:—

> O mighty son, firstborn of *Enlil [Bel]*,
> *siptu ap-lu gas-ru bu-kur ilu-Bil*

> Powerful, perfect offspring of ISARA,
> *sur-bu-u git-ma-lu i-lit-ti I.SAR.RA*

> Who art clothed with terror, who art full
> of fury!

sa pu-luh-tu lit-bu-su ma-lu-u har-ba-su

O *Ninurta*, whose onslaught is unopposed!
ilu-NIN.UR.TA [sa la im]-mah-ha-ru ka-bal-su

Mighty is thy place among the great gods!
su-bu-u man-[za-za] ina ilani rabuti

In E.KUR, the house of decisions, exalted are thee,
ina I.KUR bit ta-[si]-la-a-ti sa-ka-a ri-sa-a-ka

And *Enlil*, thy father has granted thee
id-din-ka-ma ilu-Bil abu-ka

The law of all the gods thy hand should hold!
ti-rit kul-lat ilani ka-tuk-ka tam-hat

Thou judges the judgment of mankind!
ta-dan di-in ti-ni-si-i-ti

Thou leads him that is without a leader, the man that is in need.
tus-ti-sir la su-su-ru i-ka-a i-ku-ti

Thou holds the hand of the weak, you raise him that is not strong!
ta-sab-bat kat [in-si] la li-'-a tu-sa-as-ka

The body of the man that to the Lower World has been brought down, you can restore!
sa a-na a-ra-al-[li]-i su-ru-du pa-gar-su tutira-ra-

From him who sin possesses, the sin you
    can remove!
sa ar-nu i-su-u ta-pat-tar ar-nu

Thou art quick to favor the man with whom
    the god is angry.
sa ilu-su itti-su zi-nu-u tu-sal-lam ar-his

O *Ninib*, prince of the gods, a hero you are!
ilu-NIN.IB a-sa-rid ilani ku-ra-du at-ta

I, so and so, son of, so and so, whose god is so
    and so, whose goddess is so and so,
*ana-ku pulanu apil pulani sa ilu-su pulanu
    ilu-istari-su pu-lanitum(um)*

Have bound for thee a cord, . . . [a cord]. . .
    have I offered thee;
ar-kus-ka rik-sa ku.a.tir as-ruk-ka

I have offered thee *tarrinnu*, a pleasant odor;
as-ruk-ka tar-[rin]-nu u-ri-su tabu

I have poured out for thee mead, a drink
    from corn.
akki-ka du-us-su-bu si-kar as-na-an

With the may there stand the gods of Enlil.
itti-ka li-iz-zi-zu ilani su-ut ilu-Bil

With thee may there stand the gods of E.KUR!
itti-ka li-iz-zi-zu ilani su-ut I.KUR

Truly pity me and hearken to my cries!
ki-nis nap-lis-an-ni-[ma si-mi] la-ba-ai

My sighing remove and accept my
  supplication!
   un-ni-ni-ya [li-ki-ma mu-hur] tas-lit

Let my cry find acceptance before thee!
   zik-ri [li-tib] ili-ka

Deal favorably with me who fear thee!
   si-lim itti ya-a-tu-u pa-lih-ka

Thy face have I beheld, let me have
  prosperity!
   pa-ni-ka a-ta-mar lu-si-ra ana-ku

Thou art full of pity. Truly pity me!
   [mu]-up-pal-sa-ta ki-nis nap-lis-an-ni

Take away my sin, remove my iniquity!
   an-ni pu-tur sir-ti pu-sur

Tear away my disgrace and my offenses you
  loosen!
   [i]-ti-ik kil-la-ti-ma hi-ti-ti ru-um-[mi]

May my god and goddess command me and
  may they ordain good fortune!
   [ili]-ya u ilu-istari-ya li-sa-ki-ru-in-ni-ma
   lik-bu-u damiktim(tim)

May I praise thy heart, I bow in humility
  before thee.
   [lib]-bi-ka lu-sa-pi da-li-li-ka lud-lul

THE SUMERIAN RELIGION

APPENDIX

OF LIBER-50

*A collection of esoteric supplements
released alongside Liber-50 and
as an Appendix in former editions.*

MESOPOTAMIAN MATHEMATICS : MEASURING SPACE AND TIME

Ancient Sumerians observed and understood connections between cycles, time and mathematics. In addition to the "invention" and pragmatic use of the "wheel" (or circle), they also developed "religious" calculations of the circle at 360-degrees. Their use of "Base-60" or "*sexagesimal*" math for systematic measurement of time-space remains with humanity to this present day. Consider the length of a day at 24-hours (or two sets of twelve) of "60"-minutes containing "60"-seconds each; or the celestial zones of the astrological zodiac as a "wheel" or sphere of twelve "houses" of 30 degrees each; or else the twelve 30-day "festivals of the moon" composing an annual cycle or "wheel of the year"—or "*sat-ti*." The annual year (*sat-ti*) was even originally only divided into three seasons: beginning ("*res sat-ti*"), middle ("*misil sat-ti*") and end ("*kit sat-ti*").

"Magicians" and esoteric philosophers—ancient and modern—find significance in sigil-scripts, colors, mystical alphabets and other "occult correspondences." All of these play their parts in magical ritual drama, spiritual incantations and other ceremonial applications. As a *universal* expression of "Cosmic Law," *numbers* are the most fundamental mystical "signs" in the realm of form, representing infinite wisdom and practical correspondences. Although our traditional or more familiar "classical" system of numerology is derived from a "Base-10" paradigm (for example, where "10x10=100" is a *whole*), the original Mesopotamian mathematics is "Base-6," or more appropriately, "Base-60." This only seems complicated because modern consciousness is most familiar with a "*Base-10 metric system*"—decades and centuries and "percents."

In Western civilization, "Base-60" mathematics is most closely identified with our sense of "time." Rather than dividing an hour into hundredths or percents, we are able to see 60-minutes as the "*whole pie.*" A quarter of that "pie," while still "25%"—per-*cent*, meaning "per-*100*"—it is *not* a quantified value of "25," but instead: "15," as in 15-minutes—"15x4=60." The modern standard space-measuring "foot" is divided by 12—and "12x5=60." This type of thinking more closely resembles Mesopotamian worldview.

Although school-teachers most frequently emphasize only the proverbial Sumerian "use of the wheel," it was the "mathematics" that forever established that the wheel (or more correctly, the "circle") consisted of 360-degrees—or "6x60= 360." Here among the ancients, "geometry" was born—long before the classical Greek mathematicians—a means of literal "earth-measuring."

Even more than this, the ancients demonstrated abilities to measure time-space on "earth," in the "heavens" and the relationships between.

BASIC MESOPOTAMIAN MATHEMATICAL FORMULAS

$6 \times 1 = 6 =$ earth, fire, power, spatial [*Marduk*]

$6 \times 10 = 60 =$ command, heaven-earth, fire [*Anu*]

$6 \times 10 \times 10 = 600$ chaos, void, abyss, dragon [*Tiamat*]

$6 \times 60 = 360 =$ earth-time, cycles ["*local planet*"]

$6 \times 60 \times 6 = 2160$ earth meets heaven ["*zodiacal age*"]

$6 \times 60 \times 10 = 3600$ heaven-time, spiritual cycles ["*sar*"]

A full turn or cycle of the "Wheel of the Year"—"*sat-ti*"—in *Babylonia* was separated into "12 periods" (or *zones*) of 30-days (*degrees*) each. These periods equated to 12 annual "*moonth festivals*," more appropriately called "months." The quantity values of 12x30 and 6x60 are identical—*360*. Ancient astronomers were also aware that the observed year was actually slightly longer than 360-days, and that there are actually 13 lunar cycles in a year, so an additional "*13th month*" was included to make the calculations fit the observations.

Everything is always in motion. We must even rectify the mathematics of our modern linear time-keeping with the inclusion of "leap-days." In most instances of the ancient calendar, a *"new moon"* meant the start of a *"new month."* The days counted of a month were synonymous with the "days of the moon"—for example: *"sixth day of the moon."*

SUMERIAN/AKKADIAN ANNUAL YEAR

1. Nisannu – Nisan (*spring equinox*)
2. Airu – Iyyar
3. Simanu – Siwan
4. Du'uzu – Tammuz
5. Abu – Ab
6. Ululu – Elul
7. Tishritu – Tisri (*autumn equinox*)
8. Arahsamna – Marchesvan
9. Kislimu – Kislev
10. Tebitu – Tebet
11. Shabatu – Sebat
12. Addau – Adar
13. "Second Adar" (*extra month*)

ZODIAC NAMES / THE CELESTIAL SPHERE

1. Ku-mal (*Aries*)
2. Gu-an-na (*Taurus*)
3. Mash-tab-ba (*Gemini*)
4. Dub (*Cancer*)
5. Ur-gula (*Leo*)
6. Ab-sin (*Virgo*)

7. Zi-bi-an-na (*Libra*)
8. Gir-tab (*Scorpio*)
9. Pa-bil (*Sagittarius*)
10. Su-hur-mash (*Capricorn*)
11. Gu (*Aquarius*)
12. Sim-mah (*Pisces*)

The annual cycle was also divided as a light and dark half, marked distinctly by the two primary religious festivals of ancient Mesopotamia—the spring festival of *Akitu* and the harvest festival of *Zagmuk*. Both are symbolically represented as points of "*divine marriage*" between "heaven" and "earth"—later signifying simply the relationship between a ruling King and his lands. Originally, the more popular *fertility rites* of the spring were agricultural, with an emphasis on *land renewal*. With later development and spread of these tradition, *Akitu* became known as *Ostara*—the pagan *Easter*—in dedication to Ishtar (*Inanna*).

Mesopotamian mathematics is "*sexagesimal*." The number "sixty"—attributed to Anu—is sacred within its own system, with exactly *twelve* factors —*three* of which are prime. These "factors" also appear in the tradition as *sacred* numbers—1, 2, 3, 4, 5, 6, 10, 12, 15, 20, 30 and itself, 60. It is perhaps no small coincidence that "60" is the smallest whole number value perfectly divisible by all of the numbers 1 through 6. This was very useful in the highly innovative form of "*multiplication by reciprocal*" developed by the Sumerians and Babylonians. Logic calculations requiring a value to be "divided" by another number, were instead written as a "multiplication" of the reciprocal (or inverse) of the other number. Therefore, in this system, an expression:

"60 *divided by* 10" becomes
"60 *multiplied by* one-tenth."

$[60 / 10 = 6]$ *is the same as* $[60 \times 0.1 = 6]$

Calculations of space and distance also followed *sexagesimal* patterns. Where we are familiar today with the use of centimeters and inches, feet and yards, the basic unit of length measurement in ancient Mesopotamia was essentially the division of a meter ("*kush*") into 360-parts called a *she*, each equivalent to approximately one-tenth of an inch.

If we simply transfer a decimal place, we can still use the "standard" system to visualize—where one foot or 12-inches approximately equals 120 *she*, so 1 *kush* or 360 *she* is roughly equivalent to 36-inches. [It is interesting that society has retained a system of spatial-measure where a standard unit is divided into 12-parts.]

| 6 *she* | = | 1 *su-shi* |
| 30 *su-shi* or 360 *she* | = | 1 *kush* |

The original Anunnaki hierarchy of pantheon designations runs in increments of five—from 5 to 60—allowing space for the "Olympian Twelve" to be plotted thereupon. The Sumerian Anunnaki *"Pantheon of Twelve"* of course consists of: *Anu* (60), *Antu* (55), *Enlil* (50), *Ninlil* (45), *Enki* (40), *Ninki-Damkina* (35), *Nanna* (30), *Ningal* (25), *Shammash* (20), *Inanna-Ishtar* (15), *Ishkur-Adad* (10) and *Ninhursag-Ninmah* (5).

Differences in spiritual politics for post-Sumerian Mesopotamia resulted when altering the names (or representative figures) with the "Mardukite" pantheon, but the actual "roles" themselves went unchanged—mathematically fixed. Designations for the *"Supernal Trinity"*—60, 50 and 40—become "master numbers" of Babylonian numerology. The fractional designations for the *"planetary gates"* are inherited by the "younger pantheon" in Babylon:—

1 / 2	= 30	*Nanna-Sin* (Moon)	
1 / 3	= 20	*Utu-Shammash* (Sun)	
1 / 4	= 15	*Inanna-Ishtar* (Venus)	
1 / 5	= 12	*Nabu* (Mercury)	
1 / 6	= 10	*Marduk* (Jupiter)	
1 / 8	= 7.3	*Nergal* (Mars)	
1 / 15	= 4	*Ninib, Adad* or *Ninurta* (Saturn)	

PRECESSION OF THE BABYLON GATES

1 = 7	*Nanna* – 30	30 x 2 = 60
		30 = 1 / 2 x 60
2 = 6	*Nabu* – 12	12 x 5 = 60
		12 = 1 / 5 x 60
3 = 5	*Ishtar* – 15	15 x 4 = 60
		15 = 1 / 4 x 60
4 = 4	*Samas* – 20	20 x 3 = 60
		20 = 1 / 3 x 60
5 = 3	*Nergal* – 8	
6 = 2	*Marduk* – 10	10 x 6 = 60
		10 = 1 / 6 x 60
7 = 1	*Ninurta* – 4	4 x 15 = 60
		4 = 1 / 15 x 60

INITIATION AND DEDICATION :
THE ANCIENT MYSTERY SCHOOL
LADDER OF LIGHTS

True esoteric mysteries are often earned by Seekers (and initiates of the *Ancient Mystery School*) progressively through a series of *steps*. The purpose of "grading" is to *gradually* introduce a Seeker to successively "higher" levels of realization and awareness that cumulatively unfold. Various traditions throughout the ages have each interpreted these mysteries differently, adding their own flavors and tables of correspondence, often times obscuring the number of "degrees" to fit their systems: "10 degrees" of the *Golden Dawn*; "33 degrees" of *Freemasonry*, &tc. But, the most ancient famous examples, specifically for our purposes, are described as a "sevenfold" system.

In a conventional esoteric institution, each "level" of initiation—or "step" on the "*Ladder of Lights*"—not only increases a Seeker's awareness of the system, but also grants new potential for personal development. Each "*Key*" is earned while working with a particular fragmented energy "current." These currents have also been called the "seven rays of light" (or the "seven pillars") because they comprise the main tenets of information contained within the structure of form, usually encountered directly in the physical (visible) world of light as "Cosmic Law."

Although the essential existence of the ALL is wholeness, material reality is distinguished by seven bands of a visible spectrum. Each degree appears separate—resonating its own frequency and perceived energy current. Philosophers applied this paradigm to other material spectra—*seven* notes of music, *seven* colors, *seven* days of the week—each corresponding with one of *seven* physical "celestial spheres" (*planets*), and so forth. The initiate was able to "sample" each aspect of the system in exclusion, and then as incorporated knowledge (with the rest) accumulated as a "base" of understanding—a "base" for *awareness* and *knowing*.

The Babylonian system of "*Gates,*" levels or degrees, are realized into existence uniquely by different traditions and their practices—all as a result of their *base*. Personal workings are performed from a "*Body of Light*"—the practitioner elevating their consciousness on the astral plane—then intoning specific passwords and names while tracing spiritual gate "seals," "signs" and "forms" that all trigger a preset shift in conscious *awareness* and *knowing*. These "levels" are often associated with "aethyrs" or "etheric planes" of manifestation that is deemed the "Other." Each level of initiation, step or "*rung*" requires entrance or passage through an *astral gate* equivalent to achievement of further stages of "*spiritual unfoldment.*" Similar practices are found in many modern forms of "ceremonial magic," incorporating their own "Ladder of Lights."

The Babylonian Star-Gate system—alluded to in all of the Mesopotamian influenced *Necronomicon* cycles of modern esoteric literature—corresponds with an ancient "Mardukite" plan to dedicate and seal the "younger pantheon" of the Anunnaki in Babylon under the reign of *Marduk*. These were to be the patrons of *"New-Babylon,"* a political and spiritual vision that never actually experienced total fruition, but which continues to evolve even today.

The first time Babylon fell, the main priestly class of magicians, priestesses and *Nabu*-scribes moved to Egypt, inspiring an entire "Hermetic" legacy. Modern "Dragon Court" revivals are often led by those with kinship to the Nile Region as well. This does not constitute any genetic propaganda—especially since all of the dynasties seem to switch back and forth like a pendulum swing, changing with time and politics.

Even in Babylon, we see the *"Hand of Marduk"* extend to foreign Kings when necessity demanded. By the time of the "Classical Period," Alexander-The-Great succeeded in taking control of *"dragonblood"* in Egypt, just as he had in Babylon. This over-stretched empire primed weakened conditions on a global scale, eventually leaving the known world wide open to Roman reign, particularly when the Ptolemaic dynasty was "given" to Rome by Cleopatra. Then, when Rome fell, so did its forced "false" authority systems that the world had become dependent on.

The *ankh* was widely known in Egypt as a protective symbol of life—literally the "Key of Life." Few are aware that it also esoterically represented the double-helix serpent-coiled (DNA) and *"Tree of Life"* in Mesopotamia. The *Ancient Mystery School* dedicated the symbol to the AMON-RA in Egypt (also ATEN and *"Marduk-Ra"*). It therefore became highly revered by the Mardukite priesthood altogether. In some traditions, the *ankh* was given (bestowed) to a scribe-priest-magician upon completion of their seventh (final) initiation.

The *ankh* is essentially a "cross," but also and a symbol of "crossings in the heavens"—meaning also "among the stars," or literally "the astral." In one version, the symbol is of the Self standing before the "Omega" shaped gateway. In its original Anunnaki form, this cross is drawn as a "T" (*Tau*) with a serpent being entwined around it. This is where the upper loop comes from, but which continues to coil in an "Infinity-8" pattern down the stem, simultaneously representing the famous "serpent staff" of ancient magicians. The serpent is the *"serpent of wisdom"*—the *Primordial Dragon* —and equally representing the *"Cosmic Law"* em bedded in what humans call "DNA." The Egyptian word: "AN-KH," is very similar to the Sumerian word: "AN-KI," meaning "*universe*"—the ALL—or literally: "*heaven*" + "*earth*."

It should come as little surprise that some long-standing esoteric factions of underground society —existing before the inception of the modern "Mardukite" movement—made use of these same mysteries: Egyptian Freemasonry and Rosicrucianism. These initiates hold a belief that these "stories of the gods" are in fact literal references to very ancient "luminous beings" ("*Illuminati*") that eventually *came to be* considered along the same lines as the Olympian Titans. "Tahutian" practitioners—neo-Egyptian dedicates to the embodiment of *Nabu* as the "*Thoth-current*"—still observe a (self)-initiation system inherited from the Egypto-Babylonian "*Ladder of Lights.*" This specific lore has been maintained in an occult manuscript known as the "*Crata Repoa,*" describing seven "levels" of Hermetic initiation.

* * *

A neophyte (initiate of the first degree) is called the "*Pastophoris.*" This is a title bestowed upon the Seeker who has passed the "Earth Gate," and is by nature, a Guardian of the "Gates of Men," and given the secret (pass) word: AMON. They are taught the basic symbolism of the Ladder of Lights and instruction in the physical (natural) sciences.

[Mardukite Gatekeepers: *Nanna* and *Ningal*—"*Moon Gate*." Mystical/Temple Craft: Dream Work.]

The second level is called the "*Neocoris*." The Seeker is initiated by "water and serpent" and given physical knowledge of cosmos—the mysteries of geometry, mathematics and architecture. They are bestowed with the "serpent staff," and by the password: EVE, they are granted access to the secret lore of the origins and fall of the human race. Their temple duties include cleaning the pillars (pylons) and generally tending to custodial needs of the shrines. [Mardukite Gatekeepers: *Nabu* and *Teshmet*—"*Mercury Gate*." Mystical/Temple Craft: Knowledge of Minds.]

Ascending to the third step on the Ladder of Lights earn the title of "*Melanephoris*," when the initiate becomes a Guardian of the "Gates of Death," and perhaps also given the secrets of mummification (a valuable art in Nile Region). Here, the Seeker receives the infamous "Underworld Initiation" after being led to the "Tomb of Osiris" with the passwords: MONACH CARON MINI, meaning: "I count the days of anger." [Mardukite Gatekeepers: *Ishtar* and *Dumuzi*—"*Venus Gate*." Mystical/Temple Craft: Past-Life Memory.]

From this point, the Seeker would be left in the catacombs and archives of lore to discern the secret to access the next level of initiation on their own. If they did not, they would ever remain an initiate of the third degree—but if they were to discover the "secret code," then they would be initiated as a *"Chistophorus"* via the "blindfold rite" (where a red noose is hung around the initiates neck, like a leash). Only then is he allowed to enter the Assembly of the Inner Circle, an Adept among Masters of the Highest Councils. The *"Chistophorus"* is an Adept who has earned the secret of the "shades" (a code for the "primordial battles in heaven" based on the *Enuma Elis*) and given access to the "secret chambers" of the Order. Soon thereafter, the seeker is granted an initiation by fire after proving themselves via dramatically "slaying the dragon" (or removing the head of Medusa/Typhon, etc.) and the password: ZOA. [Mardukite Gatekeepers: *Shammash* and *Aya*—"*Sun Gate.*" Mystical/ Temple Craft: History and Doctrines of the Universe.]

If successful past this point, mystical knowledge comes also in the form of a practical instruction is chemistry and metallurgy as fifth degree *"Balahate"* and the word: KHEMIA or CHEMYA. [Mardukite Anunnaki Gatekeepers: *Nergal* and *Ereshkigal*—"*Mars Gate.*" Mystical/Temple Craft: Function and Formulas of the Universe.]

After working to master the "godly" understanding of the "heavenly spheres" and the "gods of old," the Adept is the installed to the sixth degree and called the "*Guardian of the Star-Gates,*" or literally, "*Astronomer who stands before the Gate of the Gods*" (a Master-Priest status). Only then are the religious secrets divulged as well as the "true natures" of the Anunnaki, their origins and lore of their rule (and return?) on earth. The seeker is then granted another initiation through the "Gates of Death," this time to meet the Elder pantheon as a true Priest. [Mardukite Gatekeepers: *Marduk* and *Sarpanit*—"*Jupiter Gate.*" Mystical/Temple Craft: Material Unity via Love.]

The final and seventh step on the Ladder of Lights is called the "*Saphenath Pancah,*" an initiation required to attain "Prophet" status in the tradition. Secret knowledge of the gods is offered, including privileged knowledge of the "Elixir of Life." The Adept-Master-Priest, now Prophet, is given a white robe [*etangi*] and an ankh to wear. The password of the grade is: ADON ("*Adonai*"), a Semitic name, meaning "Lord of the Earth." [Mardukite Gatekeepers: *Ninurta* and *Ba'u*—"*Saturn Gate.*" Mystical/Temple Craft: Dissolution of Self via Spiritual Unity with the ALL.]

DICTIONARY OF ANUNNAKI GODS

ADAD {10}—The youngest son of ENLIL that becomes the national patron deity to the *Hittites* (called HADAD or TESHUB); possibly also recognized as BAAL HADAD in a *Hittite* version of the Supernal Trinity that is elevated to a chief god position in the same manner that MARDUK is raised in *Babylon*. As a storm god in the Anunnaki pantheon, ADAD is represented by thunder, lightning and torrents. According to Hittite records, succession of hierarchical kingship passes from ALALU to ANU to KUMARBI (ENLIL) and the BA'AL HADAD (TESHUB). In the Enki'ite (Mardukite) Babylonian system he is named ISHKUR and granted the position of *"Inspector of the Cosmos"* by ENKI.

ALALU [*"Father of the Gods"*]—The figure maintaining 'kingship' in the 'heavens' prior to ANU. An ancient *Hittite (Hurrian)* tablet cycle titled ALALU & ANU or *"Kingship in Heaven"* describes a conflict between the two for the seat of 'kingship' in the 'heavens'. The Mardukite *Tablet-K* series reprinted in *"The Anunnaki Bible"* explains: Formerly in the Ancient of Days, ALULU was reigning in heaven; and for nine *sars* did he rule the skies, but not well did he reign. Then in the ninth *sar* of his reign, ANU defeated ALULU. ALULU descended from heaven and ruled the dark-hued earth. ANU gave fight and defeated

ALULU and kingship was lowered from heaven to earth by decree of ANU.

ALULU *see* ALALU

ASAR(I)LUHI *see* MARDUK

AMARUTU *see* MARDUK

AN/ANSAR *see* ANU

ANTU {55} ["*Life of Heaven*"]—The official half-sister (by a different mother) and spouse (consort) of ANU. ANTU and ANU beget ENLIL. In archaic pre-*Sumerian* lore, ANTU is espoused to the archaic AN.

ANUNITUM *see* INANNA

ANU {60} ["*Heavenly One*"]—In the *Sumerian* Anunnaki patheon, ANU is the supreme "*All-Father*" of the pantheon; father to ENLIL by official spouse ANTU, and the father of ENKI & NINHURSAG (by other wives). Called AN in pre-*Babylonian* times and ANU by the *Babylonians*, a being whose family resides on, or emerged from the 'place of crossings' (*Nibiru*). Few of the incantation tablets (or 'prayers') invoke the powers of ANU directly, since the "heavenly force" was perceived as too vast to be channeled in its raw state, and to degrade it to anything more accessible would be to compromise the nature of what is being represented by this figure.

ANZU [*"Knower of Heaven"*]—An obscure bird-like beast/monster of an unclear nature. The ANZU or ZU usually refers to a "heavenly bird" or thunderbird that appears in an archaic tab-let cycle stealing the *'Tablets of Destiny"* from EN-LIL, disrupting the DUR-AN-KI ('Bond-Heaven-Earth') "stargate." It is possible that this half-man, half-bird, sometimes called AZAG, was a genetically engineered storm-god or artificially intelligent messenger being of ENLIL that turned "evil."

ARURU—The sister of ENLIL, alias NINTU, who is the *Babylonian* title for the 'mother-goddess' known in *Sumerian* as NINMAH or NIN-HURSAG. In the Babylonian ethnocentric epics, she assists MARDUK in creating the human race (or *'Race of Marduk'*), however, in the *Enuma Elis*, it is "blood" of KINGU that is used. Other *Sumerian* versions say the "blood" or "essence" of some other 'slain' god is used for this.

AYA [*"Dawn"*]—The official spouse (consort) of SAMAS in *Akkadian*; named SHERIDA in *Sumerian*.

AZAG *see* ANZU

BAU [*"To Accompany"*]—A daughter of ANU, who is the official spouse (consort) to NINURTA in the pre-*Babylonian* (*Sumerian*) pantheon. Her names GULA (*"Big One"*) and BAU (the sound a dog makes) are, perhaps idioms about her size/appearance. She remains a goddess in the *Babylonian* pantheon of healing (as NINTI-NUGGA).

BEL *see* EL

BUZUR *see* ENKI

DAMKINA *see* NINKI

DAMUZU *see* DUMUZI

DUMUZI ["*Son Who is Life*"]—Youngest son of ENKI and DUTTUR (a concubine of ENKI) who is the betrothed spouse (consort) to INANNA (ISHTAR) after MARDUK declines the tradition of espousing INANNA. DAMUZI is a shepherd god (as opposed to a grain deity), known as TAMMUZ in the Semitic languages. In the *Sumerian* version of the descent-cycle, INANNA descends to the *Underworld* in hopes of being its queen. When captured, she becomes a prisoner of her sister ERESHKIGAL and leaves to find someone to take her place. Upon returning to ERECH, she finds that DUMUZI has been celebrating his ascent to her throne and is not mourning for her death. Enraged, she immediately hands him over to the 'demons' of the *Underworld*. Later versions of this cycle depict the god MARDUK as somehow responsible for the death of DUMUZI and INANNA (ISHTAR) descends to the *Underworld* to release him.

EA *see* ENKI

EL—A Semitic form of the Akkadian (*Babyloni-an*) ILU or ILI, meaning '*Lofty Ones*', '*High Ones*' or '*Great Gods*'; the plural form being ILANI (or ELANI in *European Elvish-Faerie* lore), with a Semitic plural equivalent "*Elohim*", meaning liter-ally 'gods' but often used to denote the 'One God' in the Judeo-Christian *Old Testament* (which is, it-self, rooted strongly in Mesopotamian traditions). EL or BEL is also used to denote the 'Lord of the Earth-Space', or else 'ENLIL-SHIP', a position attributed not only to ENLIL (in the *Enlilite Sumerian* tradition) but also to NINURTA, MAR-DUK and even other patron deities by localized Middle Eastern cults. Later Semitic use of EL as a suffix (e.g., Micha*el*, Gabri*el*, etc.) matches the prefix use of the ILU sign in cuneiform, meaning "*Of God.*" In cuneiform, the sign is a "cross" and in later religious scriptures and rites, the literary tradition remained to place a cross before a *Divine* or saint name.

ELLIL *see* ENLIL

ENKI {40} "*Lord of the Earth*"—also known as E.A. ["*Whose Home is Water*"], firstborn son of ANU (but not the official heir), half-brother to ENLIL (heir of ANU). Also called NUDIMMUD (or PTAH in *Egypt*) meaning: "*The Fashioner*" (or "*Grand Designer*"). ENKI is the Chief scientist of the Anunnaki, taking up residence in *Eridu*, near the *Persian Gulf* and also in *Africa* (particularly *Egypt*). ENKI is father of MARDUK, begot with NINKI (DAMKINA) and is representative of the planet Neptune in the local Anunnaki 'world order'. ENKI is given control of the '*Waters of Life*' on Earth. He seeks to save his own ('*Mardukite*') legacy during the deluge and then is responsible for programing the arts and sciences of civilization into humanity. In later *Enlilite*-derived Judeo-Christian interpretations, ENKI becomes demonized as 'Satan'.

ENLIL {50} "*Lord of Air-Space*"—The official heir-son of ANU, '*Lord of the Command*' on Earth, revered as the '*God*' of Earth by Enlilite *Sumerians* and later derived Semitic (Hebrew) tradtions. ENLIL begets his own heir, NINURTA, by his half-sister NINHURSAG, but espouses SUD, renamed NINLIL and begets NANNA. In the pre-*Babylonian* paradigm, ENLIL is the Jupiter position in the pantheon that is later usurped by MARDUK. *Sumerian* tradition observes ENLIL as the 'Father' to the Anunnaki pantheon, much in the same way that ENKI is revered by the *Mardukites*. Prominent descendents of ENLIL include: NANNA, SAMAS, INANNA and NERGAL in addition to NINURTA.

ENSAG *see* NABU

ENSHAG *see* NABU

ERESHKIGAL – ["*Mistress of the Great Below*"] The Queen of the *Great Lands* in the *Sumerian* tradition, sister of INANNA-ISHTAR, granddaughter of ENLIL and spouse to NERGAL.

ERRA *see* NERGAL

GANZIR — The gatekeeper to the underworld 'Kingdom of Shadows.' The '*Gate of Ganzir*' is often confused with the '*Gate to the Abyss*' or the '*Gate to the Outside*', but instead it is a portal into the Anunnaki-controlled *Underworld*, the '*Shadowlands*' or twilight world within the domain of ERESHKIGAL, who rules this 'land of the dead'. Quoting a modern grimoire of Babylonian occultism, the "necromantic art, by which is it desirous to speak with the phantom of someone dead, and perhaps dwelling in the ABSU [*Abyss*] and thereby a servant of ERESHKIGAL... it is no less than the opening of the *Gate of Ganzir*."

GIBIL ["*He Who Has Fire*"]—The companion of the flame, a descendent of ENKI who uses fire to conduct alchemy and other feats of "*fire power*."

GIRRA—The "servant", "power" or "fire" of the 'great god'; the *Sumerian* fire-god or essence or force of a fire-god named GIBIL.

GULA *see* BAU

HADAD *see* ADAD

ILLIL *see* ENLIL

ILU *see* EL

IMDUGUD *see* ANZU

INANNA {15} ["*Lady of Heaven*"]—The *Sumerian* goddess of "passion", both 'love' and 'war', and patron of URUK, begot by NANNA and NINGAL; originally betrothed to MARDUK, she then changes her consort choice to DUMUZI. Her prowess and determination secured her a place in all ancient pantheons; being the "*Goddess of One-Thousand Names,*" titled ISHTAR in *Babylon*. INANNA (ISHTAR) is the spirit of Venus, whose day is Friday and with an essence found in copper. Her colors are green and white, significant to her domain of fertility and growth. She offers her magicians the skills in love and visions of beauty.

IRRA *see* NERGAL

ISHKUR *see* ADAD

ISHTAR *see* INANNA

KUR *see* TIAMAT

MAMMI *see* NINHURSAG

MARDUK {10/(50)} "*Son of God*"—The supreme champion of the IGIGI during the pre-

Sumerian era of the Anunnaki; heir-son of ENKI, he becomes the patron of *Babylon* and the 'Mardukite' tradition reigning for the *Age of Aries* in Mesopotamia. All tablet cycles making reference to MARDUK are purely *Babylonian* or from a direct later source, as he does not appear in any significant pre-Babylonian cuneiform tablet cycles yet unearthed. When mentioned briefly as the son of ENKI, working in *Eridu*, he is named AS-ARLUHI, becoming the patron Anunnaki "deity" of magic or 'Master of Magicians'after having inherited the craft from his father. The blatant industrious and expansive power represented by MARDUK in his ascent up the pantheon (as observed in *Babylon*) is typified by the planet Jupiter (ENLIL, by *Sumerian* standards). His color is purple.

MERIDUG *see* MARDUK

MERODACH *see* MARDUK

NABAK *see* NABU

NABIH *see* NABU

NABU {12} [*"Prophet"*]—The official post-*Sumerian* secretary of the Anunnaki, part-divine earth born heir-son of MARDUK and messenger-herald and spokesperson of the *'Mardukite'* tradition, the national cult of *Babylon* devised by NABU who assisted his father in the redevelopment of the Anunnaki paradigm (as seen in the

'*Mardukite*' religion of *Babylon* replacing the previously observed '*Enlilite*' world order of the *Sumerians*). Creating the concept of 'history' and 'propaganda', NABU gives the 'stylus' to humanity (and launches a group of scribe-priests (specially taught writing and rhetoric) to catalog the natures, identities, history and decrees (decisions) of the Anunnaki Assembly (gods) and their relationship with each other and the human ("mortal") world, thereby creating not only the first public 'religion', but the first 'mythology' (a religion rooted in literary and oral legacies of human relationships and encounters with the divine) and the systems that were able to later result (most of which are still functioning as part of 'normal' everyday life in contemporary society). NABU is the archetypal '*High Priest*' (ENSAG) of the first religion (dedicated to MARDUK) and practiced by priests who preserve the craft of ENKI in *Eridu* with science and 'magic' of the gods to power and sustain the prosperous longevity of *Babylon*.

NAMRASIT *see* NANNA

NAMMTAR *see* NAMTAR

NAMMU *see* TIAMAT

NAMTAR ["*Fate Maker*"]—The 'Black Magici-an', vizier of ERESHKIGAL in the *Underworld*, also likened to the *Assyrian (Chaldean)* plague-god NAMTARU (also the *Akkadian* word for pestilence"). From a ritual text given in *Liber 9* (Tablet-Q in *The Complete Anunnaki Bible*), the priest is to make an image of the affected (sick) person in dough [flour], so as to force the 'plague-god' that afflicts the person to come away from the body and go into the image. The ancient tablets list the name of the plague-god as NAMTARU, and in other places as URA and even URAS (in *Egypt*). In the 'Descent'-cycle, ERESHKIGAL summoned NAMMTAR, the Black Magician, saying these words as she spoke to him: 'Go, NAMMTAR, imprison her [INANNA] in Darkness, in my castle! Release against her the Seven Anunnaki Judges! Release against her the Demons of the Deep...' Then, finally, the representation of a 'demon', like the plague-god NAMTARU, was not intended for 'worship' or 'veneration' (as we might see glorified among today's misguided attempts toward 'dark paths') as a deity. Such statuary typically was constructed only to be 'ceremonially' annihilated or buried as a 'ward' against what the statue (deity) represented.

NAMTARU *see* NAMTAR

NANNA {30}—The official lunar deity of the Enlilite *Sumerian* Anunnaki pantheon, the moon-god, reigning with his feminine lunar consort, NINGAL. An Anunnaki designation of 30 is significant to the approximate number of days in a month; whereby the original Sumerian calendar consists of twelve cycles of 30 days for a 360 day year (and the reason a circle is divided into 360 degrees). NANNA and NINGAL begot the twins: INANNA and SAMAS; mythographically, the *moon* gave birth to the *sun* and V*enus* is a twin-star to the *sun*. To the ancient, the moon was the 'sun-at-night'. It illuminated the pathway for travelers and kept 'watch' as the people slept. Just as the sun is invoked to grant judgments of the daytime [see SAMAS], the moon is given domain of the night and *dreamscapes* (including the 'astral plane'). The day, "Monday", is obviously named after the moon, and is likewise sacred. The essence and color of silver is usually corresponded.

NANNAR *see* NANNA

NEBO *see* NABU

NERGAL {8}—The official spouse (consort) of ERESHKIGAL ('*Queen of the Underworld*'). NERGAL corresponds to the symbol and energetic current of *Mars,* with a fiery and destructive nature commemorated in the *Babylonian* epithet ERRA ("*Annihilator*"). The vitality and raw power of *Mars* (ruling Tuesday) is evident in the essences: iron and blood.

NINAGAL—An epithet meaning "*Prince of the Great Waters*," the name appears for a son of ENKI, who in the *Ziusurda* (*Atra-Asis*) cycle is selected by ENKI to navigate the archetypal "ark" sea-craft during the Great Flood.

NINANNA *see* INANNA

NINGAL {25} ["*Great Lady*"]—The daughter of ENKI; espoused (consort) to NANNA (SIN) and the mother of INANNA (ISHTAR) and SAMAS.

NINGISHZIDA—The 'Lord of the Tree of Life', a son of ENKI and brother to MARDUK, known as *Hermes* and *Thoth-the-Elder* (or TUTU) in a time before NABU. He is a geneticist, trained under ENKI in the arts of life engineering (and reality engineering) that was later taught by NABU (*Thoth-the-Younger* or TUTU) and it evolved into the mystical school of 'Hermetics' (or 'Hermeticism'). Having lost in the 'Pyramid Wars' (c. 3400 B.C. to 3150 B.C.) against MARDUK (RA) and not participating in the pro-MARDUK revolution of ENKI's lineage, NINGISHZIDA establishes his own realm in South America, known by the indigenous people and tradition as QUETZAL-COATL, the 'feather-ed serpent' (literally 'plumed serpent').

NINHARSAG *see* NINHURSAG

NINHURSAG {5}—The chief Anunnaki physician, the mother of NINURTA by ENLIL; a half-sister to ENLIL and ENKI by ANU. In an attempt to produce a royal heir or his own, ENKI even courts her at one time. She is not espoused to any of the pantheon, but instead serves the role of 'birth-goddess' and 'midwife' to the birth and raising of the Anunnaki children (of the Younger Generation), carrying names like MAMMI ("*Mother*") and NINTI ("*Lady of Life*"). When attempting to relieve the toiling of the IGIGI faction of the Anunnaki, ENKI seeks out NINHURSAG to assist in the 'creation' of the 'human' race. Her response, being: 'If ENKI will provide for me the clay, then I will make the creation'. In this antropogenetic cycle, she mixes the clay with the flesh and blood of 'Awmelu' (presumed to be a slain deity). In other versions, the 'essence' is more clearly semen and/or other genetic material. Cuneiform tablet records indicate that six different attempts are made before the '*Adamu*' (the seventh) is fashioned.

NINIB *see* NINURTA

NINKI {35} ["*Lady of the Earth*"]—The official spouse (consort) of ENKI, also known as DAMKINA ["*Lady Who Came to Earth*"]. NINKI is the daughter of ALALU (the 'heavenly' king prior to ANU) and the the mother of MARDUK.

NINLIL {45} "*Lady of Air-Space*"—The official spouse (consort) of ENLIL, also known with the epithet SUD ("*nurse*"). The background to the relationship between ENLIL and NINLIL is not commonly found in the typical cuneiform tablet cycles. Naturally, the lore is *not* Mardukite or

Babylonian in origin and does not appear in the tablet catalogue or commentary of (modern) Mardukite Core anthologies. The cycle is sometimes referred to as *"Enlil's Banishment to the Underworld."*

NINMAH *see* NINHURSAG

NINSHUBAR *see* NINSHUBUR

NINSHUBUR [*"Lady of the East"*]—Personal assistant (Mercury), second-in-command to the goddess INANNA (ISHTAR). She does not take a consort and there is an alluded love-relationship between her and INANNA (ISHTAR).

NINSUBAR *see* NINSHUBUR

NINTI *see* NINHURSAG

NINTINUGGA *see* BAU

NINTU *see* ARURU

NINURTA {4/(50)} *"Lord of the South Wind"*— The official heir-son of ENLIL, born of ENLIL and NINMAH, espoused to BAU. NINURTA represents the current of Saturn in the Mardukite paradigm, representative both of "hidden power" and "hidden secrets" (an idiom for the dark power and secrets behind the origins and legacy of *Babylon*). In the Enlilite *Sumerian* worldview, NINURTA (called NINIB in *Babylonian*) is the

Enlil-in-waiting, a position usurped by MARDUK proper for the *Age of Aries*. As Enlilship is typically symbolized by 'dragon-slaying', the same motif present in the elevation of MARDUK in *Babylon* rivaling the dragon-queen TIAMAT can be seen in the older *Sumerian* cycles where the prowess of NINURTA is shown in his ability to fight the mighty dragon KUR. His colors are black and violet and his essence corresponds to the metal lead.

NIRGAL *see* NERGAL

NISABA—The *Sumerian* agricultural goddess of writing and scribes; replaced by the god NABU in the Mardukite *Babylonian* Anunnaki tradition.

NUDIMMUD *see* ENKI

NUNAMIR *see* ENLIL

NUSKU ["*Bringer of Light*"]—ENLIL's vizier.

NUZKU *see* NUSKU

OANNES *see* ENKI

RAMMAN(U) *see* ADAD

SAMAS {20}—The official solar deity of the Enlilite *Sumerian* Anunnaki pantheon, brother to INANNA (SHTAR), born of NANNA and NINGAL. The sun represents the brilliance and radiant energy of life on earth; the light that allows organic life to grow and even the manner of which 'time' [and 'lifespan'] is divided. Expansive powerful energy of the solar current is invoked in magical ceremonies for general success and well-being. The fiery nature of the 'star' is called upon to 'incinerate iniquities' and reveal the nature of darkness and lies, meaning: the revelation of truth. Mistaken (by modern scholars) as monotheistic 'sun worship', solar veneration is really the celebration of life. As an archetypal representative of the 'starry' 'heavens', the sun signifies a presence and watchful eye of the 'All-Seeing-God', invoked in matters of law to bring righteous judgment. Sunday is sacred to SAMAS along with the color yellow, and both the color and essence of gold.

SARPANIT {(5)/(45)}—Seventh generation of ADAPA (by ENKI), the chosen royal spouse (consort) of MARDUK; princess-queen patron goddess (ISHTAR) of *Babylon* and mother to NABU. In alternative versions of the lore, her name ERU (or ERUA) designates her as the 'mother-goddess' of the '*Children of MARDUK*' (later associated with the light-folk or elves of Europe).

SHAMMASH *see* SAMAS

SHERIDA *see* AYA

SIN *see* NANNA

SUD *see* NINLIL

SUEN *see* NANNA

TAMMUZ *see* DUMUZI

TEHOM *see* TIAMAT

TIAMAT ["*Life-Giving Mother*"]—The 'primeval dragon' in *Babylonian* archaic epics, often equated with the *Sumerian* KUR. Later esoteric traditions associate 'her' as *Yaldabaoth* (*Ialda-baoth*) in Gnostic Hermeticism, or *Khornozon* (*Choronzon*) in Enochian Hermeticism. She is equated with the 'waters' or the 'Deep' in post-Sumerian Semitic scripture (Hebrew: *tehom*) – the all-encompassing "Sea" is parted to reveal the first 'division' (fragmentation) of "Life" in the Universe. She is paired anthropomorphically with ABZU (the *Abyss*) as the prehistoric 'ancestors' of the Anunnaki race. Her primary literary presence as TIAMAT (or T(I)AMTU) is in the *Enuma Elis* (*Babylonian*) 'Epic of Creation'. In later times, the name is used for the wife of ADAMU (*Adam*), being the equivalent to the Semitic "Eve" character.

TUTU *see* NABU

UDDU/UTTU *see* SAMAS

ZARPANITUM *see* SARPANIT

SYSTEMOLOGY
The Pathway to Self-Honesty

THE WAY INTO THE
FUTURE

A Handbook for
the New Human

A collection of writings by
Joshua Free
as selected by James Thomas

*now available as a
Collector's Edition Hardcover*

Here are the basic answers to what has held
Humanity back from achieving its ultimate
goals and unlocking true power of the Spirit
and the highest state of Knowing and Being.

"*The Way Into The Future*" illuminates the
Pathway leading to Planet Earth's true
"metahuman" destiny. With *excerpts from*
"*Tablets of Destiny*," "*Crystal Clear*,"
"*Systemology—Original Thesis*" and
"*The Power of Zu.*" You can help shine clear
light on anyone's pathway!

Carefully selected by Mardukite
Publications Officer, James Thomas,
this critical *collection of eighteen
articles, lecture transcripts and reference
chapters* by Joshua Free is sure to be
not only a treasured part
of your personal library,
but also the perfect
introduction for all friends,
family and loved ones.

(*Basic Grade-III Introductory Pocket Anthology*)

SYSTEMOLOGY
The Pathway to Self-Honesty

GO FURTHER AND BE

CRYSTAL CLEAR

CRYSTAL CLEAR

(Handbook for Seekers)

Mardukite Systemology Liber-2B
by Joshua Free

Take control of your destiny
and chart the first steps
toward your own spiritual evolution.
Realize new potentials of the
Human Condition with
a Self-guiding handbook for
Self-Processing toward
Self-Actualization
in Self-Honesty using actual
techniques and training
provided for the coveted
"Mardukite Systemology Grade-III
Self-Defragmentation Course Program"
—once only available
directly and privately from
the underground Systemology Society.

Discover the amazing power behind the
applied spiritual technology
used for counseling and advisement in
the tradition of Mardukite Zuism.

SILVER ANNIVERSARY

19 95   20 20

JOSHUA FREE

PUBLISHED BY THE **JOSHUA FREE** IMPRINT REPRESENTING

The Founding Church of Mardukite Zuism

THE JOSHUA FREE IMPRINT
JFI PUBLICATIONS

MARDUKITE
ZUISM

mardukite.com

CPSIA information can be obtained
at www.ICGtesting.com
Printed in the USA
BVHW080107140722
642138BV00011B/60

9 798986 437941